Diving into Faith

WHAT GOD SHOWED ME ABOUT FAITH, WHILE LEARNING HOW TO SCUBA DIVE

MW01007873

SYDNEY SULLIVAN

Copyright © 2021 by Sydney Sullivan

Diving into Faith

All rights reserved.
No part of this publication may be reproduced or transmitted
in any form or by any means electronic or mechanical, including photocopy, recording,
or any information storage and retrieval system now known or invented,
without permission in writing from the publisher, except by a reviewer who wishes
to quote brief passages in connection with a review written for inclusion
in a magazine, newspaper, or broadcast.

Paperback ISBN: 978-1-09835-792-4
eBook ISBN: 978-1-09835-793-1

Printed in the United States of America

Dedication

This book is dedicated to my wife and everyone in the world who truly within their heart want to be stronger within their faith

Table of Contents

Faith in God is better than worry in your heart.
I gave God my life and He showed me what living really is.

Introduction

There are over 6 million active scuba divers worldwide and one brand new one in me just one year ago. Scuba diving is something that I always wanted to do but did not have the time or the budget to accomplish. Growing up, I would see all the greatest action heroes scuba diving in uncharted waters, swimming with all the intimidating creatures of the deep. Watching a lot of Discovery Channel and National Geographic throughout my life always inspired me to one day take the leap into learning and pioneering the ocean blue in the safest ways possible, to explore all the underwater phenomena and wonders that most don't ever get to see. When I joined the military, I met all kinds of people who went scuba diving for pleasure, profession, or sport. Going into the depths of a world uncharted, free flowing and separated from the daily one I lived in, was always something that interested me.

Tobi diving off Florida Reef in Key Largo, Florida

This uncharted world has millions of things to explore, intriguing creatures to meet, and dangers to maneuver. It has beautiful landscapes, vast depths, and endless opportunities to explore. When I initially arrived in Key West, I knew that it would be the opportunity, the opening I was finally looking for. But by this time, I was married and had young children. It was daunting to think about how an injury or even worse could affect my family. Regardless, you cannot expect your dreams to become a reality while remaining on the sidelines.

Faith is a lot like this underwater world. To move in faith, we have to be able to look past the uncertainty of any given situation. We must be willing to move through beautiful waters, choppy waters, and the dangerous storms that we charter in life's ocean. Learning, discovering, exploring, growing in a new aspect of faith every day when we dive into our individual lives. Faith is a vehicle we drive...as we travel the highways of our lives. We fasten the seatbelt and press the gas. The question becomes, are you moving forward or in reverse? Pedal to the metal or just put putting along? Or has life convinced you to sideline your faith in the break lane?

We all have our battles over how we handle what life presents to us, but our faith is the anchor that keeps us grounded to God during rough seas. If we look at stories within the Bible, we see numerous examples of faith. Faith tears down walls, gets us to places God has promised, leads to redemption, conquers cities. Miracles take place and can be a mighty stimulus for transformation. That's the plan as you submerge yourself in this book: to dive into topics that will further illuminate God's message about faith, how we activate faith, and what operating in faith looks like.

Descriptions of Faith

- *allegiance to duty or a person*
- *complete trust or confidence in someone or something.*
- *fidelity to one's promises*
- *strong belief in God or in the doctrines of a religion, based on spiritual apprehension rather than proof.*
- *firm belief in something for which there is no proof*

The general definitions above are not the foundational platform from which the core concepts I write in this book have derived. Faith is a lot deeper than these mere descriptions provided above. It is more multi-faceted than we realize. It is more than just believing in God, but rather the believing in the word of God and grasping the full understanding of what the word promises to His people. You cannot have faith without complete trust. My father used to say to me whenever

I missed a shot in basketball, nearly hit a home run, or came close to winning, that *"almost"* does not count. And *almost* faith does not count either. Jesus did not *almost* die on the cross for humanity. You were not *almost* born. You don't *almost* breathe the oxygen around you. Do not be an *almost* believer. Jesus addressing the Pharisees in Matthew 12:30 says, "Whoever is not with me is against me." You either have faith or do not have faith. There is no grey area. Many would argue, why believe with no proof? No hard-hitting evidence of what is believed for. And as humans we are built as such. We want to know the conclusion before we start. We want to know what is my return on investment out of the deal.

The return on investment is what God deems as necessary for the circumstance. He is the beginning and the end. That said, the return is not always for you. Your investment may benefit somebody else. If at the end it is for the glory of the God's Kingdom, that should be enough for all of us. And if it is not, I would question what place is your faith based from? But if we believe in what God says and challenge our confidence in Him, we have all the proof we need to move forward in any situation. God's track record speaks for itself bar none. Faith is giving your last (Mark 12:41-44) to God and trusting God within your circumstance.

Faith is a daily and at times arduous journey. When belief is tested, that is when faith has an opportunity to triumph. If the goal is to get to eternity with the Father, faith is the vehicle that delivers us there. Belief gets us in the car, and faith takes us the rest of the way. And this is an oversimplification of the elements that come together as faith. Ford forged cars through assembly lines; God forges our faith through the power of who He is. Complex subject matters look simple when peering in from the outside. And that's how I was exposed to scuba diving. I thought it a simple product just by looking at the end result and found it to be more dynamic and intricate then what was presented at face value.

I experienced many amazing things while learning to scuba dive, and God showed me some amazing points about faith that will remain with me for the rest of my life. Although this book does not include GoPro footage, this message will provide enough HD picture to encourage and unlock your faith forward. Let us dive deeper together and further mature our faith. Diving is an action. Faith is an action. Let us remain committed today to be more action-oriented in our faith. Be more proactive to pray and believe. And less reactive to the problems that spontaneously manifest themselves before us. Let's dive into our faith.

Seeking in Faith

Hebrews 11:6

*"And without faith it is impossible to please God,
because anyone who comes to him must believe that he exists and that he
rewards those who earnestly seek him."*

The verse above begins with the word "without," the absence of or lack of presence. Without faith it is impossible even for Tom Cruise to please God. And it all stems from belief. The Greek word for belief is *pisteuō*, to be committed to. We commit ourselves to hundreds of things on a daily basis. Maybe we're committed to waking up early, committed to our children, committed to our craft, committed to our daily routines, committed to our alma maters, committed to our sports teams, committed to sending emails, committed to checking social media, committed to spending time on our phones, committed to conversations, committed committed committed. There are a lot of things that are fighting for our commitments every second of the day. And yet to have faith you must be committed in your belief. A commitment is a continual obligation to or seeking of something or someone. And in the verse above if we are not committed to believing in God, it is impossible to please God. The second part of that verse is the justification, because anyone who comes to him must believe that He exists and that He rewards those who earnestly seek Him. And through this justification we must first believe, which is wrapped up in our faith and only rewarded in our faith when we earnestly seek Him.

To be earnest is to be in an intense and serious state of mind. Intense: an impressive degree or amount. God wants you to seek after Him intensely. At an extreme degree or great zeal. He wants you to give all you are to seeking Him. This is important because anyone who has done this level of seeking, we tend to recognize for their passion for what they do. And a lot of times we say these people are over the top because their aspirations are excessive. When was the last time your faith was excessive for Christ? When we see someone in the Olympics, we say that person must have been extremely dedicated to get there. When we see amazing singers, artists, professors, business people, speakers, athletes, military members, we praise them for their commitment towards the greater goal whether they are excessive or not. But God says He rewards those who are continually seeking after Him. Do people see you for your earnest attitude towards God? Do they testify about your extreme dedication to faith? Can you be honest with the Father and say you are serious minded about the Kingdom and your relationship with Christ? And yet I wonder how many of us have Olympic-size dedication in our faith.

Once I landed in the Florida Keys, I sought out diving. No one had to twist my arm or hold a gun to my head to force me to research, talk about, and seek out what it took to become dive certified. I traveled to different dive stores, explored many companies, and asked many questions in pursuit of my ultimate goal that faith would pay off. I even prayed about it multiple times. I wonder how God feels and views our will to seek the immense number of things we do in our daily lives as compared to the amount of faith we put in seeking Him. We should seek to be better, reach, and achieve, but it all should come through Christ. He knows the desires of our hearts. But first we must seek Him.

Hebrews 11:8-10; By faith Abraham, when called to go to a place he would later receive as his inheritance, obeyed and went, even though he did not know where he was going. By faith he made his home in the promised land like a stranger in a foreign country; he lived in tents, as did Isaac and Jacob, who were heirs with him of the same promise. For he was looking forward to the city with foundations, whose architect and builder is God.

When I go diving, I don't know how things are going to turn out. I don't know what I am going to encounter, see, or feel through the process. Every dive is different because the ocean is a fluid place that changes every second. God called Abraham. He did not know how it was going to turn out or where he was going. Abraham left what he knew, for what God knew. In faith he made his home in another place far removed from what he was accustomed to. But he was looking forward as we do when we seek. We are always looking for what comes next. What God has in store. I may not know, but I am going where God is taking me. After over a decade in the military, I know people who enlist or commission to serve their country to end up right back where they are from originally. Sign up, just to go back home. And that's OK, but I emphasize leaving what you know is not always the easiest thing. And Abraham left what he knew to seek what God had.

9

Left what was in his hands for what God was holding for him, and all of us are blessed through Abraham's obedient faith.

Hebrews 11:13-16; *All these people were still living by faith when they died. They did not receive the things promised; they only saw them and welcomed them from a distance, admitting that they were foreigners and strangers on earth. People who say such things show that they are looking for a country of their own. If they had been thinking of the country they had left, they would have had the opportunity to return. Instead, they were longing for a better country—a heavenly one. Therefore, God is not ashamed to be called their God, for he has prepared a city for them.*

I love this verse because we have all these goals and dreams that we seek after, we "welcome them from a distance." We welcome things that have not yet come into our lives. We continually dive deeper in order to get to what we strongly desire. And here God is showing us through the writer of this text in Hebrews that this is what faith really is…welcoming all that God has in store for us at a distance. We are not in the promise currently but ever moving towards it. Ever looking and walking forward in our belief of the promises God has already set in our lives and eternity. Seeking past even earthly outcomes to the eternal rewards God has for us in Heaven. But first we must earnestly seek.

Faith is striving for a life change. Faith is not just believing what comes next or what will work out but actively seeking to be transformed and renewed in our thinking, in our walks, in our daily journeys. What good is it to keep going through life without growing, without experiencing the fullness of what God offers, without maturation? Diving was a life-changing experience for several reasons. It was out of my comfort zone, it gave me a new vantage point that I now get to use daily, and it grew me closer to God through all of the overwhelming, beautiful things He has shown me. The opportunity to see more pushes me more to understand who God is even though I still cannot fully understand His greatness and sovereignty.

Chapter 1

*"Very truly I tell you Pharisees, anyone who does not enter
the sheep pen by the gate, but climbs in by some other way, is a thief
and a robber. The one who enters by the gate is the shepherd of the sheep.
The gatekeeper opens the gate for him, and the sheep listen to his voice.
He calls his own sheep by name and leads them out. When he has brought
out all his own, he goes on ahead of them, and his sheep follow him
because they know his voice. But they will never follow a stranger;
in fact, they will run away from him because they do not recognize
a stranger's voice." Jesus used this figure of speech, but the Pharisees did
not understand what he was telling them.*

*Therefore Jesus said again, "Very truly I tell you,
I am the gate for the sheep."*

John 10:1-7

The Gatekeeper

When I initially signed up for the scuba certification, I knew that there
was a classroom portion and a pool course to enhance our knowledge
and teach the appropriate skills to be successful within the ocean. I

figured that I would show up, and they would tell me everything I needed to know, the class would test, and after passing the test we would be on to the pool—the steak and potatoes of the deal. Looking back at the experience, it was a poor assumption on my part. Scuba Schools International (SSI), the vendor I went through, has an online course prep feature before you arrive. When I signed up, I was currently in a new job, plus taking courses in my master's degree, and with the family tied in the mix I had little time to study much of anything, plus only four days to go through it all. Since the class portion was three hours, I figured I'd let the pieces fall where they did. Plus, I usually pick-up things quickly anyway; how hard could it be? (Famous last words.)

At 0630 I stepped into my driveway on a beautiful sunny Friday in Key West, inventoried my dive equipment, and left. I picked up Sergeant Boynton from his house at 0700 and made the trip out to the dive center. Once there we met Christian, who was going to be our instructor for the duration of the three-day course. Christian was a proud Texan and had been diving since he was in his teens. He had been instructing all over, including in Malaysia. We eventually went through the three-hour course. Christian was very intimate and thorough with the dive material. He was very good at sharing realistic lessons as they pertained directly to the dive experience and sharing his own stories as well. Low and behold, it was exam time.

Christian stated it would be a fifty-question test, mentioned some preliminary administrative details to write down, and off we went. There were some things on the test that I know for sure we covered in the course and others that were apparently in the online course guide. Not having looked at 97 percent of the course guide, I was feeling much like a teen in high school who didn't study for the pop quiz. We turned our sheets in and Boynton was the first to be graded.

"92 percent," shouted Christian. Boynton had successfully made it through! Now it was my turn. As I watched him grade my paper, every red X on the sheet made my heart sink. I knew I didn't know all the answers but I thought I knew most of the questions that I came across? He looked up at me and the look said it all and then he said, "78 percent." He said, "You need an 80 percent to pass." Christian went over the ones I got wrong and explained the reasoning behind the answers. He then issued another test and this time I passed! I was so relieved! All the testing was done and I could focus on the practical training. Or so I thought.

Christian dismissed us for lunch and we ate at the bar that was attached to the dive shop. I had the biggest burger they had on the menu and some fries. Why do I mention such a fact, you ask? Well, let us continue further. At the end of lunch, Christian met us and told us we had another test. Boynton and I looked at each other and laughed—Christian was a big joker, so we naturally assumed he was kidding. He said, "No, I'm serious. You have to take two tests in the pool before you can continue with the course." Then the cheeseburger in my stomach began to laugh. And my excitement turned to anxiety as to what kind of test awaited me in the pool. We changed into swim trunks and met Christian at the pool with all of our gear. Once there he said, "You have two tests. The first is you have to do fourteen laps down and back in under twelve minutes. The second is you have to tread water for ten minutes. Let me know when you guys are ready!"

WHAT! I have always been a decent swimmer but it had been a long, long time since I worked out in the pool. Plus, I'd never swam for time before! This was becoming a problem fast. Either way I was already in the pool and had paid my money, so I really had no choice but to pass these tests. We stretched, took our marks on the south side of the pool, and waited for Christian's signal: "GO." Boynton and

I shot out the gates. Boynton kept track of the laps we completed. Boynton was like a fish in the water, and I was behind him by a whole body-length. With every touch of the wall, every kick, every splash, every stroke, I just kept pushing myself to make the time. We got to the end and successfully made time. I was out of shape! I felt like I'd just done some sprints and my muscles were all tight from the exertion. Christian gave us some good time to recover, then it was time to tread water for ten minutes. With my body feeling like I just did a solid workout, I was hoping I had some leg strength to get the job done. We went to the ten-foot side of the pool and Christian kicked off the time. I decided to spark some conversation about random topics to take my mind off the situation. Take my mind off being nervous. And it worked! After talking about David Goggin's new book, treading techniques, and other random things, before we knew it the time was up and the time for assessments had passed. Another amazing relief!

The rest of the day was spent in the water practicing and rehearsing scuba-diving fundamentals. Christian was very attentive with every instruction given from the equipment, to the movements in the pool, to hand-signals. At 1800, after everything was prepped and squared away for the next day, Boynton and I left the dive shop. We would return mid-day the next day for our first scuba-diving adventure, on the reefs of the Florida Keys.

So why go through all the trouble of explaining what occurred during the first day? In retrospect it can come off as a very routine course of action for an experience for scuba diving. But in relation to faith, it opens another lens from which to glean. John 10 is a great for the path we will walk in this approach to faith:

"Very *truly I tell you Pharisees, anyone who does not enter the sheep pen by the gate, but climbs in by some other way, is a thief and a robber.*

The one who enters by the gate is the shepherd of the sheep. The gatekeeper opens the gate for him, and the sheep listen to his voice. He calls his own sheep by name and leads them out. When he has brought out all his own, he goes on ahead of them, and his sheep follow him because they know his voice. But they will never follow a stranger; in fact, they will run away from him because they do not recognize a stranger's voice." Jesus used this figure of speech, but the Pharisees did not understand what he was telling them.

Therefore, Jesus said again, "Very truly I tell you, I am the gate for the sheep. All who have come before me are thieves and robbers, but the sheep have not listened to them. I am the gate; whoever enters through me will be saved. They will come in and go out, and find pasture. The thief comes only to steal and kill and destroy; I have come that they may have life, and have it to the full.

The Kingdom of Heaven is like us earning the privilege to scuba dive in open water from a broad point of view. How so? Christian was the gatekeeper. He taught us, tested our knowledge, and tested our endurance in the pool, and our application of what was taught. Isn't a little bit of this starting to sound like how Christians should be living? I mentioned earlier that SCI opened an online course as soon as I registered. That is a lot like reading your Bible. Christians sign up to follow God, and the word of God is the rubric that we are to be diving from daily. This gives us the information on how to live and interact with others daily. Just as the online source supplied the ins and outs of how to dive safely and the dangers to watch out for. The Bible does the same thing, but how many believers actually read? Honestly, just as I neglected the online course material, how many Christians live based on their own knowledge, words passed along (hearsay), or broken context? It is important to take the time to know what God has really promised you, who He is, and how that is practical to what you are getting yourself into by following Christ. And because of our deceptive disregard and lack of investment, when we are tested, the gateway for things like insecurity, depression, addiction, fear, and over-confidence prevail instead the foundational attitudes, behaviors, and mindsets God wants us to have as we swim through life's currents. Like our instructor Christian did in the course, God provides all the answers through talking with us daily when we open ourselves up to the dialog with Him, but even more so in THE WORD that He has given us beforehand.

All the assessments that I had to do just to be allowed to practice diving in the pool are like the trials we encounter daily. The assessments are a testament to our ability to persevere despite the temptations or the pitfalls we put ourselves in operating naturally. Jesus never promised an easy road. As a matter of fact, the Bible says that it is the Matthew 7:13: "Enter through the narrow gate. For wide is the gate and broad is the road that leads to destruction, and many enter through it. But small is the gate and narrow the road that leads to life, and only a few find it." We will endure the tests of this Earth by grinding through the road map the word of God lays out for us. We can get through the suffering and through the challenges, however insurmountable they may seem with perseverance.

Perseverance

James 1:12; *Blessed is the one who perseveres under trial because, having stood the test, that person will receive the crown of life that the Lord has promised to those who love him.*

2 Peter 1:3-9; *His divine power has given us everything we need for a godly life through our knowledge of him who called us by his own glory and goodness. Through these he has given us his very great and precious*

promises, so that through them you may participate in the divine nature, having escaped the corruption in the world caused by evil desires.

For this very reason, make every effort to add to your faith goodness; and to goodness, knowledge; and to knowledge, self-control; and to self-control, perseverance; and to perseverance, godliness; 7and to godliness, mutual affection; and to mutual affection, love. For if you possess these qualities in increasing measure, they will keep you from being ineffective and unproductive in your knowledge of our Lord Jesus Christ. But whoever does not have them is nearsighted and blind, forgetting that they have been cleansed from their past sins.

Suffering

1 Peter 5:10; *And the God of all grace, who called you to his eternal glory in Christ, after you have suffered a little while, will himself restore you and make you strong, firm and steadfast.*

1 Peter 4:1; *Therefore, since Christ suffered in his body, arm yourselves also with the same attitude, because whoever suffers in the body is done with sin.*

Luke 14: 27; *And whoever does not carry their cross and follow me cannot be my disciple*

And although we go through these tests and phases, it is important to know that God is with us the whole way. Our instructor never left us during the tests, and neither will God. And we don't always pass, but we do learn. I didn't pass my first diving written test, but with more instruction I was able to exceed my previous score and become more knowledgeable. This ultimately helped me more practically apply the concepts and be more aware of the all the movements that take place in the pool and ocean. Jesus is the gatekeeper but He wants to give us guidance, not be some general deterrent from Heaven. As stated before in John, "*The sheep listen to his voice.*" If I didn't listen to Christian, I would have failed the exam, would have not been successful in the pool with the dive equipment, could have possibly hurt myself or someone else, and would never have gotten my certification. Does this sound familiar? When we do the opposite of what God is saying, doesn't it sound like some of the consequences listed above?

The pitfalls of going against God leave us in the murky waters of the world trying to maneuver without a guide, without a friend, without a way out. We end up hurting ourselves, others, and not maximizing the potential God has laid out for us. We delay what's destined, set back success, and ruin the riches God has for us. We are not perfect. We all mess up. We all slip up. God is perfect. And by chasing His perfection we experience His excellence along the way. Our faith becomes stronger along the way. We dive deeper in our relationships along the way. Things become clearer. We become separated from binding strongholds. Diving into faith sounds nice, but faith takes action. Our choices condition our actions and customs. What will you choose? Persevere, or permeate in what the world gives you. The ocean is an enormously large place that can be beautiful, frightening, and mysterious. But I'd rather dive in with the One who created it, not the one who is set to destroy it. Remember, your faith is matched by your fortitude to move forward.

Romans 8:37; *No, in all these things we are more than conquerors through him who loved us. 38 For I am convinced that neither death nor life, neither angels nor demons, neither the present nor the future, nor any powers, 39 neither height nor depth, nor anything else in all creation, will be able to separate us from the love of God that is in Christ Jesus our Lord.*

A prayer of faith

God, open up my faith.

Open my heart to believe in things unseen that have been promised by your word.

Allow all your strength, might, power, and spirit to flow in my life and create a life change like never before.

I bring myself into your presence to be changed radically by you and to fortify my courage moving forward.

I love you, thank you for everything you have given and will continue to provide

In Jesus name,

Amen

Pool vs the World

Like I mentioned earlier, scuba divers in training usually spend a day in a pool to learn all the basics before the techniques are performed in the water. And this makes sense. Before a parent takes a teenager on the open road, they usually take them to an empty parking lot to not injure themselves, other riders in the vehicle, or any drivers on the road. Same in principle here. Diving is an extreme sport. Why? Because everything you do and how you respond to every situation and manage your equipment can have a direct impact on keeping you alive. Thus, the pool day. In addition, in the pool you are safe. If there is a problem, you are never too deep to pop up to the surface and discuss what went wrong. This is not always the case in a real-world diving scenario. The tools that are given in the pool are intended to equip you in an ever-changing environment. The pool is safe, and it is safe for a reason. The visibility is clear. It is a controlled environment with no waves, currents, debris, or animals. The wind and weather are not factors, nor are so many other elements that have an opportunity to transpire in open waters.

Why is this relevant to faith? Just as the pool is safe, ideally, the church is a safe place. We fellowship there, worship, teach, preach, pray, bring our kids, share, and learn in this space, all for God's glory. We have the opportunity to practice our faith continually within the confines of these facilities. Which is an awesome thing and, may I add, critical. Just as the pool shows a diver how to thrive and survive in their relationship with their equipment in the water, so does the church show Christians how to survive and thrive through their relationship with Christ in the open waters of the World. Just as the diver has tools, so does the believer. The pool is an ephemeral place; it's a transition point, a temporary space. The Church, in the physical sense of a building, is a transitional place, not the end all be all. What is the point of diving if we never leave the pool? The point of diving is to explore all of the underwater phenomena that are out there! The pool frames for the reality you are going to encounter. The Church propels us to live in the world but not of it. As the body of Christ, the spiritual church, we take Christ into the world through us.

On a daily basis, we navigate the open waters of our daily lives... kids, relationships, divorces, suicide, job loss, job gain, athletics, depression, healthy living, finances, and so much more. We need a safe space, but we need to realize that space is God and not use the church as a crutch. We need to get out of the pool as Christians and help the World see Jesus through everything that God provides us, using the tools we learned in the pool to better dive daily into the waters of the world. We all have access to God, we have the ability to pray for one another, and we all have the word as believers. But do we take these tools outside of our pools? Outside of our safe spaces? Outside of our Churches? Outside of our homes? When God has called us into the world to bring people closer to Him, why at times are we reluctant to express and share our zeal with others as Christians, or Live one way in the Church and another in the World?

How then shall they call on Him in whom they have not believed? And how shall they believe in Him of whom they have not heard? And how shall they hear without a preacher? And how shall they preach unless they are sent? As it is written:

"How beautiful are the feet of those who preach the gospel of peace, Who bring glad tidings of good things!"

But they have not all obeyed the gospel. For Isaiah says, "Lord, who has believed our report?" So then faith comes by hearing, and hearing by the word of God.

Romans 10:14-17

Just as anything else, it can be daunting moving from a safe place to one that is unpredictable. Moving to a place where outcomes are not expected or anticipated. And that's OK. What is not OK is standing still but moving forward in faith as we grow towards God. I get it. Jesus can be counter cultural. Especially in a world full of currents pushing and pulling their own directions. Our faith is not built on fear. So, as we move from pool to open water however routinely, we understand that it is God moving us out the pool in waters in which He will not let us sink through the power of His word and presence in our lives. We must be willing to leave the pool for the things that are greater. Both for us and His glory.

And we know that God causes all things to work together for good to those who love God, to those who are called according to His purpose.

Romans 8:28

What pool are you in?

Chapter 2

Circumstances are the curriculum God uses to teach us

The Journey

Staff Sergeant Boynton and I arrived at the dive shop the next day around 0715 to prepare for dives three and four of our certification. Anxious and excited, we prepared our gear and got everything on board the boat for the trip out to the reef. This was an early dive, in contrast to the day before, when we dove in the middle of the day. And it is important to mention the day before was a cloudless, bright, sunny, eighty-degree day. Today was a seventy-five-degree and cloudy day. The visibility was bad the first day and with the clouds being all overcast I was sure that the visibility down below the ocean was going to be messy, especially since it rained hard the night before. But nonetheless we were here, ready to go for the experience and open up the doors for more to come in the potential future.

The boat made its way out through the one-mile seaweed-green canal with big white houses on both sides with their own docks and boats. We got to the sea at the end of the canal and although it was overcast outside, there was a split over the ocean with us in the middle. On the east side of the boat five miles away we could see the rain coming down from dark clouds, and from afar it looked like a dark blueish-purple shower curtain draped over the ocean. And to the west was the very same thing. I looked down at the water and it was choppy with a dark emerald-green tint to it. Every time the boat jumped, the gap between the three- to four-foot waves was apparent. I mean, it felt as though the boat flew for a second or two! I felt out of my element, not necessarily in danger, but the conditions weren't ideal.

At the moment I felt as though I was in one of those *movies*. *"The Perfect Storm"* type of movies, the type where maybe I shouldn't stick around for the climax of the film to take place. The visibility under the water was bad the first day we went out and, in my mind, I was sure it'd be worse with these conditions. I figured it would make me a better diver, but it didn't ease my mind about what I couldn't see while in the water if that was the case. With sharks, barracuda, jellyfish, Moray eels, man-o-war, and other things lurking, I wanted all the visibility I could get. Then it began to rain on the boat as we got closer to the dive site. I was literally telling myself, *Lord, what did I choose to get myself into!*

I'm sure that's how many of us feel when we are called to things that are initially given in grandeur, glamour, and glory. Right! What happens when God gives you the vision but the process doesn't look like the promise? What happens when the trip is turbulent but what was promised to you looks like everything you ever wanted? When the thing that has been placed deep down in your soul doesn't look like what you envision. When current circumstance doesn't reflect projected anticipated outcome. What happens then? When the trip doesn't feel like the turnout. What are you going to do?

Collection of dive tanks as we launch to our dive site in the Keys of Florida

Joseph was given visions when he was a young man, dreams that reflected a high position he would ultimately hold in another country. A position that raised him to a place of authority past his older brothers. The future tribes of Israel. Joseph was given a beautiful turnout but not the trip that it would take to get there, a trip that was catalyzed by anger from his brothers, slavery, and prison. Joseph's trip to the glory God had in store for him was turbulent. It was rough, choppy, and full of storms—much like I mentioned before and like many of us may experience on our way to the glory God has called us to live. Although we may be in a troublesome situation, that doesn't mean God is missing or made any mistakes. God was with Joseph when he excelled and as a slave under Potiphar.

Genesis 39:2-6; *The Lord was with Joseph so that he prospered, and he lived in the house of his Egyptian master. 3 When his master saw that the Lord was with him and that the Lord gave him success in everything he did, 4 Joseph found favor in his eyes and became his attendant. Potiphar put him in charge of his household, and he entrusted to his care everything he owned. 5 From the time he put him in charge of his household and of all that he owned; the Lord blessed the household of the Egyptian because of Joseph. The blessing of the Lord was on everything Potiphar had, both in the house and in the field. 6 So Potiphar left everything he had in Joseph's care; with Joseph in charge, he did not concern himself with anything except the food he ate.*

Genesis 39:20-23; *Joseph was thrown into prison for a crime he didn't commit. Another storm and hard waters to navigate for anyone, and yet God was still with him on the path forward.*

Joseph's master took him and put him in prison, the place where the king's prisoners were confined. But while Joseph was there in the prison, the Lord was with him; he showed him kindness and granted him favor in the eyes of the prison warden. So the warden put Joseph in charge of all those held in the prison, and he was made responsible for all that was done there. The warden paid no attention to anything under Joseph's care, because the Lord was with Joseph and gave him success in whatever he did.

And even as we navigate the turbulence of the journey, God will allow our gifts to blossom as we stay faithful to Him! Everything that God has given you will develop and grow the more connected you are to God. Joseph is locked up in prison and there in the midst of the situation we see God work through Joseph to interpret the dreams of the cupbearer and the baker imprisoned with him (Genesis 40). This is vital; in spite of the uncontrollable situation Joseph seems to be in, we see God is in control of the situation. We are able to see the bread crumbs that are foreshadowing the bigger destiny God has planned for Joseph.

It is important to broach that Joseph had high hopes at this time that his interpretation would possibly have secured his freedom within a short time frame, but as seen in the text, Joseph doesn't arrive in front of pharaoh for another two years. It is necessary that our faith not be singed and burnt up by our frustration, anger, sadness, or other emotions that may stem from our lack of understanding. While sitting in prison for another two years, another 730 days, Joseph could have easily given up on God! How easily do we fall away from God when we become frustrated or feel victimized in some way?

2 Peter 3:8-9; *But do not forget this one thing, dear friends: With the Lord a day is like a thousand years, and a thousand years are like a day. The Lord is not slow in keeping his promise, as some understand slowness. Instead he is patient with you, not wanting anyone to perish, but everyone to come to repentance.*

Proverbs 16:9; *"In their hearts humans plan their course, but the Lord establishes their steps."*

God's timing is not our timing. This must be differentiated and separated. We all have our expectation, but God is the one who orders the steps! When Joseph was finally brought in front of the Pharaoh to interpret the dream, Joseph's reply was, "I cannot do it." Joseph replied to Pharaoh, "but God will give Pharaoh the answer he desires"(Genesis 41:16). It was God that provides the answer. It is God that will provide the clarity to what's burdening you. Joseph still gave credit to God and understood where the source of understanding came from. In heart of problems lean on patience and prayer. As my brother Kevin Hill says, put the onus on God. Give it all to God and master your faith to enable your ability to persevere when things become cumbersome. Joseph interpreted the dream and was put in charge of the palace and all of Pharaoh's people! Later, his position brought the opportunity for his entire family to be united and live in the country of Egypt.

Could your journey that God has called you on bring opportunities today and in the future for others because of your obedience and fortitude?

Can your decision for God today be an opening for someone else tomorrow to see how great God works?

When the turbulence doesn't look like the turnout, what will you do?

Sully diving off the Florida Reef in Key Largo, Florida

Chapter 3

Planning is the sheet music to execution's symphony

Plan Your Dive, Dive Your Plan

Puddling down the one-mile canal, sitting down towards the back of the boat next to all the dive tanks, I had a whole bunch of thoughts about what day one in the ocean would bring. As we got a fourth of the way down the canal, the divemaster onboard called everyone to the back of the boat, where I was stationed. The other two trainee divers sat down as well as two Navy divers. The divemaster was a charming midwestern guy in his early sixties named Ron. Ron had been diving for decades, always wore a pair of sunglasses that didn't block the sun entirely, and was quite charismatic. The divemaster hunkered himself down on the middle platform in the center between all of us.

Ron commenced, "Alrighty, it's a beautiful day to dive today and hopefully the visibility will be nice during your dive today! The most important thing for you to do as a diver is have a plan before you go out anywhere and stick to that plan. This is called 'plan your dive, dive your plan.' So that is what we will be doing today and the following days every time before we arrive at the reef. Now, if I hold my hand out with my knuckles towards the sky, this is what the reef looks like from above. The reef looks like a hand with its fingers spread out with the knuckles being the back walls of the reef. Between the fingers are the pits or lanes between the reef you will be swimming in. My knuckles are north and the ends of the fingers are south. If you go too far past the end of the finger reef, you will be able to tell because there will be nothing but sand around you.

"There will be plenty of wildlife because this is a no fishing reef. The reef is protected, so the fish are naturally curious and unafraid of visitors. Make sure you have a buddy and are aware of where the boat is at all times. You will have between one hour and fifty-five minutes of dive time before you need to be back on the boat to move to the next part of the reef. When the time is getting close, I will hit the metal ladder with a metal object. Underwater you will hear a loud ‹tink, tink, tink, tink› noise. That will be your signal to head back if you haven't done so already. Because the reef is protected, we need to be good stewards of our environment by not touching any of the coral out there. Try to be safe, try not to break any of the coral on the reef, and do not remove anything from the ecosystem you may have found while diving. Other than that, it is a beautiful day, the water is seventy-six degrees, and we should have a great time once we arrive out there!"

This is very exciting and crucial for moving forward with momentum in our faith. Why? How many of you have ever done something without a plan and it didn't pan out so well? How are we planning out our lives through the faith we have in Christ? With our faith we too should have a plan and stick with that plan. We should have our system in place. Our faith must have a strategy. We should plan our dive, dive our plan. It has a framework to work within. Allow me to further plunge deeper into this concept. Just as Ron gave all the rules of engagement, God has given us a plan in Christ as an example as to how we are to dive daily within our faith and in this world.

Prayer

Jesus would always begin His day with God. He would continually find quiet, isolated places to pray to convene with the Father.

Mark 1:35; *Very early in the morning, while it was still dark, Jesus got up, left the house and went off to a solitary place, where he prayed.*

Are you communicating with the master diver before you swim out into the waters of the world? Before you take on the beautiful or stormy days, are you consulting with the master diver? Ron gave us all the tid-bits and jewels as to how we should maneuver on the reef. Do you believe God can do this, too? The Master Diver of all creation can provide the insight to the situation He already is aware of. You haven't dived yet, but He already knows the waters.

Proverbs 3:19-20; *By wisdom the Lord laid the earth's foundations, by understanding he set the heavens in place by his knowledge the watery depths were divided, and the clouds let drop the dew.*

It is not only important, but the lifeline of your life hinges on the relationship you build with God.

Jesus also prayed for others. He prayed for forgiveness for those who put Him on the cross. He prayed for His disciples. He teaches us how to pray in Matthew 6:5-13:

And when you pray, do not be like the hypocrites, for they love to pray standing in the synagogues and on the street corners to be seen by others. Truly I tell you, they have received their reward in full. But when you pray, go into your room, close the door and pray to your Father, who is unseen. Then your Father, who sees what is done in secret, will reward you. And when you pray, do not keep on babbling like pagans, for they think they will be heard because of their many words. Do not be like them, for your Father knows what you need before you ask him.

"This, then, is how you should pray:

Our Father in heaven,

hallowed be your name,

your Kingdom come,

your will be done,

on earth as it is in heaven.

Give us today our daily bread.

And forgive us our debts,

as we also have forgiven our debtors.

And lead us not into temptation,

but deliver us from the evil one."

If I have questions about where I am going, I ask the divemaster. Part of the definition of a divemaster is having supervision or responsibility over a group of divers. And as the body of Christ, does God not have supervision over us? Over all things? Who has supervision over your life? This may be a reason why we feel lost: because we are governing ourselves under the wrong supervision.

Obedience

Jesus was obedient to His calling and to the commands that were set before Him. Although Jesus was without fault, He still had John the Baptist baptize Him. Although He was tempted after a forty day and forty night fast, Jesus wasn't swayed by the devil's attempts. Although the weight of the crucifixion pressed on Him in the Garden of Gethsemane, Jesus remained faithful to the tasks. There are multiple things I can list, but really, it's about what are those things in your life that beat against your obedience to stay with the plan? What are the things that come up to pulverize your perseverance? Crush your commitment to the plan. Hebrews 4:15 tells us, "For we do not have a high priest who is unable to empathize with our weaknesses, but we have one who has been tempted in every way, just as we are—yet he did not sin." How much more should we have confidence in remaining obedient to God's will in our lives. That the roadmap we are following has been tested and true. Our obedience is a reflection of who the master diver is. I would point out that your obedience to a way of living, course of actions, and attitudes reflects that master diver you follow. The characteristics of your choices reveal whose service you reside under.

"Faith is only real when there is obedience, never without it, and faith only becomes faith in the act of obedience."
—Dietrich Bonhoeffer

Serve

To serve is to gain. Jesus served the Father by serving others in various ways; teaching, healing, praying, encouraging, obedience, prophesying, and giving. Christ used all these avenues to serve others and display what it means to walk in God's light. Jesus went to where he was called and serve the need there. Jesus taught everywhere he went. Taught crowds of thousands and down to individuals. On more than one occasion, he would educate religious leaders that tried to kill Him, teaching them on more than one occasion about how they should be living out the law and their relationship with God. He gave His time, His heart, His wisdom, food, miracles, and all of who He was to God and allowed that to flow to the people that encountered Him. Jesus, being all who He was, ate with those considered sinners, washed the feet of those that followed Him, and sat with those deemed unworthy in society.

Romans 12:6-8; *We have different gifts, according to the grace given to each of us. If your gift is prophesying, then prophesy in accordance with your faith; if it is serving, then serve; if it is teaching, then teach; if it is to encourage, then give encouragement; if it is giving, then give generously; if it is to lead, do it diligently; if it is to show mercy, do it cheerfully.*

It's similar to how some people may be able to tread water for long periods of time, some swim faster than others, some can hold their breath for long durations, and some have endurance. But how do you serve others with the gifts that God has given you. Within the kaleidoscope of talents that have been given unto you, how are you multiplying them unto God and His Kingdom?

Humility

Be humble in what you do. Although you may have great successes in life, humility can be the cobblestone on your path forward. More importantly, in our relationship with God. My stance is humble when I approach God. We have all been sinners and made mistakes: "For all have sinned and fall short of the glory of God"(Romans 3:23). But the Bible speaks of Humility:

Proverbs 11:2; *When pride comes, then comes disgrace, but with humility comes wisdom.*

Proverbs 22:4; *Humility is the fear of the LORD; its wages are riches and honor and life.*

And we see this displayed in Jesus continuously throughout His ministry. We see His humility to serve in light of the fact that He is the Son of God, and the word of God in the flesh. He was superior to us yet had the humbling capacity to serve and showcase how we should serve God daily. Every time a conversation arose to point fingers at Jesus, Christ responded in His submissiveness to the Father. All credit went to God above for the things that took place;

John 5:19; *Jesus gave them this answer: "Very truly I tell you, the Son can do nothing by himself; he can do only what he sees his Father doing, because whatever the Father does the Son also does.*

John 5:30; *By myself I can do nothing; I judge only as I hear, and my judgment is just, for I seek not to please myself but him who sent me.*

John 5:41-44; *I do not accept glory from human beings, but I know you. I know you do not have the love of God in your hearts. I have come in my Father's name, and you do not accept me; but if someone else comes in his own name, you will accept him. How can you believe since you accept glory from one another but do not seek the glory that comes from the only God?*

John 6:38-40; *For I have come down from heaven not to do my will but to do the will of him who sent me. And this is the will of him who sent me, that I shall lose none of all those he has given me, but raise them up at the last day. For my Father's will is that everyone who looks to the Son and believes in him shall have eternal life, and I will raise them up at the last day.*

John 7:16-17; *Jesus answered, "My teaching is not my own. It comes from the one who sent me. Anyone who chooses to do the will of God will find out whether my teaching comes from God or whether I speak on my own.*

John 7:29; *Then Jesus, still teaching in the temple courts, cried out, "Yes, you know me, and you know where I am from. I am not here on my own authority, but he who sent me is true. You do not know him, but I know him because I am from him and he sent me.*

John 8:28-30; *So Jesus said, "When you have lifted up[a] the Son of Man, then you will know that I am he and that I do nothing on my own but speak just what the Father has taught me. The one who sent me is with me; he has not left me alone, for I always do what pleases him." Even as he spoke, many believed in him.*

John 8:42; *Jesus said to them, "If God were your Father, you would love me, for I have come here from God. I have not come on my own; God sent me."*

John 14:10; *Don't you believe that I am in the Father, and that the Father is in me? The words I say to you I do not speak on my own authority. Rather, it is the Father, living in me, who is doing his work.*

John 14:24; *Anyone who does not love me will not obey my teaching. These words you hear are not my own; they belong to the Father who sent me.*

Living and operating in a state of humility is the freedom from pride and arrogance. Have you been shackled, incarcerated by self-regard and pridefulness to the point of actually not receiving fully what God has stored for you? If Christ, who knew God intimately, was sent from God, and was perfect in all manners tested, then how much more in our faith should we challenge ourselves to kneel down subjugated to God's will for us; "Now faith is confidence in what we hope for and assurance about what we do not see" (Hebrews 11:1). And although we may not see God directly or know what is to come, we have faith, believe, and are humble to experience the wonders that are given daily.

The world culture teaches us daily to focus on ourselves. Look at who we are individually. If this wasn't the case, our phone cameras wouldn't be designed with selfies in mind. It is important for you to look at who you are in Christ. God alone created you and knew who you were before you were born. I believe most would agree that it would be irresponsible of me to walk into the scuba-diving school and act like because of my self-indulged athleticism it would be easy for me to accomplish the course. I would have quickly been made a fool of. Just as a baby cannot boast of feeding itself with a bottle, neither should we rest in the false flattery of things that will not last beyond this lifetime. In the same light it is foolish for us to remain in a state of deep pleasure and self-satisfaction with the person in the mirror rather than the one we should be aiming to mirror daily. Jesus said Himself, "by myself I can do nothing." And Philippians 4:13 says, "I can do all things through Christ who strengthens me." The key is through Christ, but the culture teaches us on our own accord. We are given the perception that we (ourselves) are successfully cemented in the notion of prior achievements. But all that we achieve striving for God is stored in heaven for us. Everything we do for God's Kingdom is in front of us versus what has been done.

Philippians 3:7-14

But whatever were gains to me I now consider loss for the sake of Christ. What is more, I consider everything a loss because of the surpassing worth of knowing Christ Jesus my Lord, for whose sake I have lost all things. I consider them garbage, that I may gain Christ and be found in him, not having a righteousness of my own that comes from the law, but that which is through faith in [a] Christ—the righteousness that comes from God on the basis of faith. I want to know Christ—yes, to know the power of his resurrection and participation in his sufferings, becoming like him in his death, and so, somehow, attaining to the resurrection from the dead.

Not that I have already obtained all this, or have already arrived at my goal, but I press on to take hold of that for which Christ Jesus took hold of me. Brothers and sisters, I do not consider myself yet to have taken hold of it. But one thing I do: Forgetting what is behind and straining toward what is ahead, I press on toward the goal to win the prize for which God has called me heavenward in Christ Jesus.

Forgiveness

Matthew 18:21-35

Then Peter came to Him and said, "Lord, how often shall my brother sin against me, and I forgive him? Up to seven times?"

Jesus said to him, "I do not say to you, up to seven times, but up to seventy times seven. Therefore, the Kingdom of heaven is like a certain king who wanted to settle accounts with his servants. And when he had begun to settle accounts, one was brought to him who owed him ten thousand talents. But as he was not able to pay, his master commanded that he be sold, with his wife and children and all that he had, and that payment be made. The servant therefore fell down before him, saying, 'Master, have patience with me, and I will pay you all.' Then the master of that servant was moved with compassion, released him, and forgave him the debt.

"But that servant went out and found one of his fellow servants who owed him a hundred denarii; and he laid hands on him and took him by the throat, saying, 'Pay me what you owe!' So his fellow servant fell down at his feet and begged him, saying, 'Have patience with me, and I will pay you all.' And he would not, but went and threw him into prison till he should pay the debt. So when his fellow servants saw what had been done, they

were very grieved, and came and told their master all that had been done. Then his master, after he had called him, said to him, 'You wicked servant! I forgave you all that debt because you begged me. Should you not also have had compassion on your fellow servant, just as I had pity on you?' And his master was angry, and delivered him to the torturers until he should pay all that was due to him.

"So, my heavenly Father also will do to you if each of you, from his heart, does not forgive his brother his trespasses."

We experience hardships, blindsided by life, and the bumpy bomboras of bungled relationships. It is easier to be angry and bitter than forgive as we have been forgiven first. As we follow our divemaster Christ, we too emulate Him in following the guidance he leaves before in the forgiveness of others. This is the beauty of what God has given us through Christ. When we are disgusted, appalled, and unmoved at times by the heinous or even subtle sins, offenses, or mental lapses, realize that it is natural to feel that way. We have shared the same light when we were in our sins. And Jesus in all his perfectness was ripped apart before the foundations of the World to cover the sins of everyone. Forgiveness, mercy, and love all at once. How can we follow behind our divemaster? How do we not only reflect the same values God has shown humanity but what He is calling us to daily?

Forgiveness in Compassion

Joseph was thrown into slavery by his own blood. Joseph's own brothers gave him over to slavery. After that he spent an estimated seventeen to twenty-one years in Egypt in slavery, as a prisoner, and then as an overseer over Egypt. That is a lot of time for the opportunity to allow bitterness, hatred, and anger to settle in. But Joseph had faith in

God, God worked on Joseph, and God showed favor to him over the course of many hardships. Joseph was confronted with one of the biggest emotional decisions of his life. He had been raised to the highest place only second to the pharaoh after twenty some odd years.

Genesis 41:37-44

So the advice was good in the eyes of Pharaoh and in the eyes of all his servants. And Pharaoh said to his servants, "Can we find such a one as this, a man in whom is the Spirit of God?"

Then Pharaoh said to Joseph, "Inasmuch as God has shown you all this, there is no one as discerning and wise as you. You shall be] over my house, and all my people shall be ruled according to your word; only in regard to the throne will I be greater than you." And Pharaoh said to Joseph, "See, I have set you over all the land of Egypt."

Then Pharaoh took his signet ring off his hand and put it on Joseph's hand; and he clothed him in garments of fine linen and put a gold chain around his neck. And he had him ride in the second chariot which he had; and they cried out before him, "Bow the knee!" So he set him over all the land of Egypt. Pharaoh also said to Joseph, "I am Pharaoh, and without your consent no man may lift his hand or foot in all the land of Egypt."

Then his brothers show up on the scene (Genesis 42). I can only imagine the mixed emotions Joseph must have felt when seeing his brothers. Betrayal, anger, hate, love, a desire for family connectedness, and, I am sure, many others. Yet once Joseph revealed himself, it was compassion he showed his brothers. Joseph knew what he was called to in service through God and the people. The past had been now placed in the present. In forgiveness we see the compassion Joseph showed his brothers and provided them abundance amongst a famine. They thrived when the greater land was trying to survive. Compassion connects us to the heart of God and opens others to a glimpse of what God has in store for them. Our reflection of his forgiveness opens others for an opportunity to feel God's love and see how God is moving in our lives through our daily faith.

Forgiveness in Patience

John 8:2-11

At dawn he appeared again in the temple courts, where all the people gathered around him, and he sat down to teach them. The teachers of the law and the Pharisees brought in a woman caught in adultery. They made her stand before the group 4 and said Jesus, "Teacher, this woman was caught in the act of adultery. In the Law Moses commanded us to stone such women. Now what do you say?" They were using this question as a trap, in order to have a basis for accusing him.

But Jesus bent down and started to write on the ground with his finger. When they kept on questioning him, he straightened up and said to them, "Let any one of you who is without sin be the first to throw a stone at her." Again he stooped down and wrote on the ground.

At this, those who heard began to go away one at a time, the older ones first, until only Jesus was left, with the woman still standing there. Jesus straightened up and asked her, "Woman, where are they? Has no one condemned you?"

"No one, sir," she said.

Then neither do I condemn you," Jesus declared. "Go now and leave your life of sin."

Jesus is the master of patience. One of His many nicknames is the Prince of Peace. Jesus within this context, intention was to teach. And teach he did through the disturbance and hidden agenda of religious figures. As he was being probed by question after question Jesus tempered his response in patience. Even though the Pharisees were there to undermine who Jesus was. Jesus knowing full well what the intentions of their hearts were, and still responded in kind to the principle of the matter rather than their immediate actions. Sin is sin. Whether it is adultery, a white lie, murder, stealing, manipulation, lustfulness, and more.

"For God did not send His Son into the world to condemn the world, but that the world through Him might be saved"(John 3:17). Understanding that we all have sinned; we do not lie in judgment of others but temper ourselves with patience as God has patience with us all. We do not all get it right all the time. But we strive to do the right things and fall accountable on the things we do not. It is God who judges and forgives the sins of all mankind. We should prayerfully check our disposition with those who have fallen short of glory as we all have.

Matthew 18:21-35; *Then Peter came to Him and , how often shall my brother sin against me, and I forgive him? Up to seven times?"*

Jesus said to him, "I do not say to you, up to seven times, but up to seventy times seven…So My heavenly Father also will do to you if each of you, from his heart, does not forgive his brother his trespasses."

We get so caught up on the act itself at times that we forget to treat the sin. We should treat the person with patience and love as Christ does each of us. Please do not misunderstand me. "Then neither do I condemn you," Jesus declared. "Go now and leave your life of sin." The object is to leave sin, not to keep repeating the same means of disobedience over and over again. God's forgiveness is a gift. God's patience is a gift. We as the body of Christ should do our best through guidance of the Spirit to reciprocate these gifts. I do not ever want to be on the receiving end of the reciprocity earned from continuous disobedience. Temper your emotions and treat the sin with patience, wisdom, and counsel from the Lord.

How can you better be in tune with your relationship with God as the divemaster?

How will you better plan your daily dives in faith?

What things are distracting your attention from God or the dive plan?

Chapter 4

Things become clearer, when the mask is flooded with God

Blurred Expectations

So, diving off of the Keys, you would expect the water to be super clear all the time, but the reality is that it is not. You really don't know the visibility of the water you are diving into until you get there. And this is a great pausing point for reflection before we continue. The majority of us have expectations for things that we have never undergone, never experienced, or never had before. For example, marriage. Many people have an idea and expectations for what their marriage will be like, but for those who have been in a marriage longer that five minutes, let alone decades, there begins to be some delineation, modifications, and challenges as the dynamics of the relationship shift. As an athlete headed into competitions, I have had my share of expectations or assumptions going into games and tournaments, but those change very rapidly and I along with teammates have had to adjust on the fly.

Sully diving off Marker 32 in Key West, Florida

Many people have presumptions about going to church based on particular worldviews, historical experiences as children, or hearsay. These are just crude examples; others include buying a home, dealing with death, walking into a new job, becoming a parent, school, becoming financially responsible, and the list goes on. We have all been in the boat of presumption. Here's the thing, though: if we are busy assuming what will take place, then we miss the opportunity of what would have taken place. If we are making every move based on assumption, then we are not truly walking in faith. We are taking the opportunity from God to show us something miraculous for our lives when we make the "calls" of what we "think" will happen.

So now that we have addressed that, let us continue forward. Once anchored into the first dive spot, the instructor diver was the first to jump into the water. He jumped in, popped out of the wave, and called us one by one into the three- to four-foot waves sloshing around us. This being the first dive, our nerves were jolting, anxiety was setting in, and the moment of truth was upon us. With all my gear on, I walked to the edge of the side of the boat. There was a steel ladder that I had to step onto off the edge of the boat. I stepped down, and the divemaster was holding on to my tank. I looked at the horizon in front of me, my right hand on my goggles that were over my face and regulator and my left hand behind my head to ensure my mask didn't fall off. Then I take took one giant step forward, four feet down, and splashed into the murky ocean.

The two seconds I was submerged, I looked down and could see nothing below me but a dusky green salty water. I immediately swam to the surface. It felt like the entire world was moving, and for me it was. I felt like the rubber toys my kids play with in the bathtub, just whisking around and bobbing to and fro. I gave the "OK" sign to the divemaster and proceeded to swim near the instructor. Now, here's where it gets fun. Once all divers were in the water, we swam over to a red buoy that was hinged to the anchor on the sea floor. Before continuing, I must explain that there are two types of visibility, horizontal and vertical. Our visibility all around that day was eight to ten feet, which is pretty horrible when diving. Our instructor's motto seemed to be "If you can learn to dive in low vis, you can dive in any visibility."

At this point it was our time to descend to the bottom, which was thirty to forty feet down to the ocean floor. Remember, I mentioned earlier that I saw nothing when I looked down before. So in my mind there was no telling what I was going to descend onto once I started sinking towards the bottom. I could land on coral, some random school of fish, anger some barracuda, a turtle, hopefully not a shark, or whatever was below! The time came and we were to descend holding onto the anchor line towards the bottom. So down I went, not really knowing how fast I was descending, just my eyes on the instructor's head below me. Suddenly a huge coral wall came out of nowhere right below me at about twenty feet down, and I swerved forward as quickly as I could to avoid breaking any coral, let alone getting stung by some fire coral or sea urchin. With ten feet left to descend, I very quickly got to the bottom, in twenty seconds kneeling in a bed of sand, surrounded by fifteen- and ten-foot walls of coral, and a reef teeming with a chalk full of sea life. I felt like I landed on Jupiter or Mars, an untouched ecosystem that looked as though it had been there before the dinosaurs.

As I said, the visibility was low. When I glanced up from the floor I could easily see where the light was coming from, but it was all still very blurry. Anything that was beyond ten feet was a blurry shadow or unseen completely. Sitting there at the bottom, I quieted my mind. Being in the ocean is a different type of quiet. There are faint sounds and you actually hear the movement of the water. Not only was I in unfamiliar territory, but I barely had awareness of my surroundings. I was cut off from water that lay beyond my given scope. In that moment I closed my eyes and prayed to God at thirty feet: "God, you are in control. I do not understand all that is going on, but you do. Show me what you have called me to see."

You see, we are all called to something. The truth of the matter is when you are called to it and you get there, you will have the confidence in God to allow Him to show you what you need to see. We need to manage our expectations and not reflect them as if they are God's. God's will, will shine through when we don't trade ours for His. I could have allowed the cloudy, foggy depths to shift my mindset off of the experience. Immediately, jumping into the water was uncomfortable mentally, off-setting physically, emotionally unbalanced, but I never let it take control of me spiritually. I was locked in on God, so even when I was taken down through the waters and couldn't see a thing until twenty feet, I had the faith to continue. I believe God has gone ahead of me, so I must throttle my expectations and allow God to work when environments or situations are outside of my control. But we will talk about control another day. When we move within the construct of faith, God can take us to depths far beyond what's imagined.

He turned a shepherd boy last in his family into a king…

David was the youngest of seven brothers. When Samuel was called to anoint someone, David was not immediately around. He was out in the field tending to the sheep. And God took that same shepherd boy to shepherd a nation.

1 Samuel 16:7-13

But the Lord said to Samuel, "Do not consider his appearance or his height, for I have rejected him. The Lord does not look at the things people look at. People look at the outward appearance, but the Lord looks at the heart."

Then Jesse called Abinadab and had him pass in front of Samuel. But Samuel said, "The Lord has not chosen this one either." 9 Jesse then had Shammah pass by, but Samuel said, "Nor has the Lord chosen this one." Jesse had seven of his sons pass before Samuel, but Samuel said to him, "The Lord has not chosen these." So he asked Jesse, "Are these all the sons you have?"

"There is still the youngest," Jesse answered. "He is tending the sheep."

Samuel said, "Send for him; we will not sit down until he arrives."

So he sent for him and had him brought in. He was glowing with health and had a fine appearance and handsome features.

Then the Lord said, "Rise and anoint him; this is the one."

So Samuel took the horn of oil and anointed him in the presence of his brothers, and from that day on the Spirit of the Lord came powerfully upon David. Samuel then went to Ramah.

Shake Prisons...

Paul and Silas, wrongfully beaten and jailed in Philippi, did the unimaginable and began worshipping God. They were in a bleak situation, having just been given lashes and put into the inner most part of the prison, and began praising God.

Acts 16:26-33; Suddenly there was a great earthquake, so that the foundations of the prison were shaken; and immediately all the doors were opened and everyone's chains were loosed. And the keeper of the prison, awaking from sleep and seeing the prison doors open, supposing the prisoners had fled, drew his sword and was about to kill himself. But Paul called with a loud voice saying, "Do yourself no harm, for we are all here."

Then he called for a light, ran in, and fell down trembling before Paul and Silas. And he brought them out and said, "Sirs, what must I do to be saved?"

So they said, "Believe on the Lord Jesus Christ, and you will be saved, you and your household." then they spoke the word of the Lord to him and to all who were in his house. And he took them the same hour of the night and washed their stripes. And immediately he and all his family were baptized.

There are times when we, like Paul, are called into such situations. We do not always see the outcome, but we are called to be there. Our confidence is cemented in God. Through the beatings, through the fire, through the challenges, through the blur, we step towards the one who can give all clarity. The obedience through the fray saved the life of the jailer and brought Christ to his family.

Open up oceans...

Moses was leading Israel out of Egypt and literally got caught between a sea and an Army.

Exodus 14:11-12; *Then they said to Moses, "Because there were no graves in Egypt, have you taken us away to die in the wilderness? Why have you so dealt with us, to bring us up out of Egypt? 12 Is this not the word that we told you in Egypt, saying, 'Let us alone that we may serve the Egyptians?' For it would have been better for us to serve the Egyptians than that we should die in the wilderness."*

This was a blurry position for the Israelites but not for Moses. The stuttering and confident, lacking Moses who was at the burning bush, had become a very different person at this point. And despite the visibility of the situation, his faith transcended what was in front of him.

Exodus 14:13-21

And Moses said to the people, "Do not be afraid. Stand still, and see the salvation of the Lord, which He will accomplish for you today. For the Egyptians whom you see today, you shall see again no more forever. The Lord will fight for you, and you shall hold your peace."

And the Lord said to Moses, "Why do you cry to Me? Tell the children of Israel to go forward. But lift up your rod, and stretch out your hand over the sea and divide it. And the children of Israel shall go on dry ground through the midst of the sea. And I indeed will harden the hearts of the Egyptians, and they shall follow them. So I will gain honor over Pharaoh and over all his army, his chariots, and his horsemen. Then the Egyptians shall know that I am the Lord, when I have gained honor for Myself over Pharaoh, his chariots, and his horsemen."

And the Angel of God, who went before the camp of Israel, moved and went behind them; and the pillar of cloud went from before them and stood behind them. So it came between the camp of the Egyptians and the camp of Israel. Thus it was a cloud and darkness to the one, and it gave light by night to the other, so that the one did not come near the other all that night.

Then Moses stretched out his hand over the sea; and the Lord caused the sea to go back by a strong east wind all that night, and made the sea into dry land, and the waters were divided.

Heal Sickness...

A Centurion. A warrior. A man of authority within the Roman Army. His servant that was close to him was sick and ready to die. Despite his position, despite the condition of the circumstance, the Centurion's belief was bigger in Jesus than any experience had told him in the past.

Luke 7:6-10 NKJV; *Then Jesus went with them. And when He was already not far from the house, the centurion sent friends to Him, saying to Him, "Lord, do not trouble Yourself, for I am not worthy that You should enter under my roof. Therefore I did not even think myself worthy to come to You. But say the word, and my servant will be healed. For I also am a man placed under authority, having soldiers under me. And I say to one, 'Go,' and he goes; and to another, 'Come,' and he comes; and to my servant, 'Do this' and he does it."*

When Jesus heard these things, He marveled at him, and turned around and said to the crowd that followed Him, "I say to you, I have not found such great faith, not even in Israel!" And those who were sent, returning to the house, found the servant well who had been sick.

We set our expectations through our faith, not faith through our expectations. By putting our faith in God, the expectations our boundless. We should never put our limit on a God that is supremely powerful. The Scripture says, "He marveled at him..." "I have not found such great faith in Israel!" Wouldn't it be something to wow God with your faith, just floor Jesus with your belief?

Prayer under pressure...

Everything was going amazing for Daniel. I mean amazing! He had the favor and heart of King Darius, the King of Babylon. Daniel held a prestigious position of rule within the Kingdom and was so trustworthy that even those who were jealous of him could not find any fault with Daniel. Following the Lord comes with its share of unforeseen circumstances.

Daniel 6:6-9; *So these administrators and satraps went as a group to the king and said: May King Darius live forever! The royal administrators, prefects, satraps, advisers and governors have all agreed that the king should issue an edict and enforce the decree that anyone who prays to any god or human being during the next thirty days, except to you, Your Majesty, shall be thrown into the lions' den. Now, Your Majesty, issue the decree and put it in writing so that it cannot be altered—in accordance with the law of the Medes and Persians, which cannot be repealed." So King Darius put the decree in writing.*

The Bible says that when Daniel heard this, he continued to serve God without hesitation. Without a blink of an eye Daniel continued to pray. And he didn't just pray in the closet, behind closed doors, in the bathroom, in the basement or the attic. Daniel opened the windows and prayed three times a day. If that wasn't enough, Daniel didn't complain, cry, yell, or breakdown, but rather gave thanks to God. In the immediate crossroads of the presented juncture, Daniel continues forward through the unsettled environment and lodges himself onto the foundations of God!

Daniel 6:10; *Now when Daniel learned that the decree had been published, he went home to his upstairs room where the windows opened toward Jerusalem. Three times a day he got down on his knees and prayed, giving thanks to his God, just as he had done before.*

What happens next is well known but not always well understood…

Daniel 6:16; So the king gave the order, and they brought Daniel and threw him into the lions' den. The king said to Daniel, "May your God, whom you serve continually, rescue you!"

Even the king acknowledges how dedicated Daniel's faith was, his belief, his servitude is to God. And it's amazing that what seems unknown to us was known to everyone the entire time. There was no denying who Daniel served. In the times of success. In the times of intense adversity. The consistent nature of Daniel's submissiveness to God came first. Too many times we allow other things to come to the forefront of our situation, instead of the God who is bigger than it. Daniel's relationship with God was more important than possible emotions or self-preservation. When the outcome seems invisible, our faith brings God to become more visible within every breathe of our situation.

Daniel 6:19-23

At the first light of dawn, the king got up and hurried to the lions' den. When he came near the den, he called to Daniel in an anguished voice, "Daniel, servant of the living God, has your God, whom you serve continually, been able to rescue you from the lions?"

Daniel answered, "May the king live forever! My God sent his angel, and he shut the mouths of the lions. They have not hurt me, because I was found innocent in his sight. Nor have I ever done any wrong before you, Your Majesty."

The king was overjoyed and gave orders to lift Daniel out of the den. And when Daniel was lifted from the den, no wound was found on him, because he had trusted in his God.

God will reveal mysteries and the gaps in your heart. It is a matter of releasing what you expect to happen and allowing God to walk you through what He has called to happen. I was expecting clear waters and a line of sight as far as my eye could see. But that's not what I got. I got a limited panorama that left me with a decision to make: lean on God and learn from the experience at hand, or submerge myself in a state of fear, frustration, or completely turn off into my own reservations.

Although things may seem limited in the situation, we must know that God is limitless. When God has His eyes on all that is going on, my job is to only look at Him.

Clear Your Mask

Kneeling on the sandy, pebbly, crushed coral floor at thirty feet, it was quiet but a different quiet. My eyes closed; the sounds of the ocean were all around. You could hear the ocean moving! You could hear the clicks of the dolphins in the distance and the waves, and it was a cool seventy-five degrees at the bottom. I opened my eyes, and my mask was blurry. I believed it was just super murky since the visibility was low, so I didn't think too much of it. I saw the instructor in front of me and I figured I had a cheap mask that just didn't give me the clarity

I was hoping for. Then the instructor pointed to me and asked me to clear my mask. Clearing your mask underwater as a diver is essential so that if any water floods your mask you are able to rid your mask of it to improve your sight. Subsequently, I went to clear my mask by bending my head back forty-five degrees towards the surface and blew air out my nose for three seconds. Amazingly my mask was full of salt water and I was surrounded by the beauty of the coral walls, barracuda, big grouper, yellowtail snapper, and other elements of a diverse eco-system.

We often operate under the presumption that we have full visibility within our lives, that we can see everything that is going on, when a lot of times we are actually clouded by the things surrounding our lives. What would happen if we allowed our masks to be cleared by God? What if we allowed God into our lives in such a way that we were shown some things that may have been in front of us the whole time? What does it look like when God is given the control to cleanse our lives? It looks like pure revelations and new insights to what really needs to be seen. It looks a lot like removing saltwater from your goggles and seeing all the beautiful things God has created in the world. It looks like what life should be instead of what we think it is. It looks like when we invite Jesus into our lives. It's removing all the cloudiness, the dirt, the filth, the sin, the addictions, the guilt, the shame, the bitterness, the anger, the anxiety, the everything that lays over what the truth really is for what God has in store for you—what He REALLY HAS IN STORE FOR YOU!

We have to be able to tilt our heads back and allow God to work in us, and those things will fall away the more we allow Him in. It's like athletes and dieting. The more you eat the right foods and drink the right stuff over a long period of time, the more the craving for the fatty stuff goes away. There are times the cravings and temptations come back, but you must stay the course. The worst thing that can happen to a blind person who just got their eyesight is to go back to being blind—to go back to not seeing all the wonderful colors, nature, and the phenomenal wonders of the world. To go back to a world of darkness and bleakness. I have had challenging times within my military career, ministry, athletics, marriage, parenthood, academics, family, and the list continues. The worst thing that can happen in any challenge is not having the clarity to find a solution or see a way out. It compounds the frustration and tension of the situation. But God is that dive instructor just sitting in front of us waiting on us to clear our mask with Him so that we may swim into the glory in store for us.

Simon the sorcerer is an example of removing the fog. In Acts 8 we see that the people and Simon thought he was great because of the magic he performed. The Bible says he amazed the people of high and low for a long time. But when Philip and John came along Simon believed, was baptized, was astonished by the miracles he saw, and followed the two disciples everywhere. God is good for taking the blinders off. Good for initiating the defoggers on our windows for us to see the truth about what is actually in front of us. Jesus does this with the Samaritan woman by the well in John 4 when He confronts her. He breaks down the dividing walls between cultures, personal narratives, social statures, and perception. God sees who you are but, more importantly, He wants *you* to see *Him* daily.

The real question is, do you want to see? So many become accustomed to the fog in their "mask" and wish to accept the blurry haze they have been given or built up. Some do not wish to get the clarity for fear of what they will see and the revelation of where they are. But wherever you are, God will make Himself available. That's the beautiful thing about all of this. God, Jesus met us where our sin was and will cleanse it from you! Do you want to get away from the haze?

Let's be honest: how much as believers, as Christians, do we need to have our mask cleared? Even when we know what God is capable of and we meddle in complacent mindsets, routines, and lack relational ministry—when our ideas, fervor, mindsets, and passion for God become continually sedentary—our gifts have become stationary because we have become comfortable with the lens we have adopted at the level of relationship with Christ. We see Thomas in the book of John doubt the disciples seeing Jesus after He had been crucified; "Unless *I see the nail marks in his hands and put my finger where the nails were, and put my hand into his side, I will not believe"(John 20:25)*.

This man had walked with, eaten with, slept around, and seen everything Jesus had done. He had seen the miracles, the power of the word, the blessings, lessons, controversy, the healings, all God was in Jesus. He had been called by Jesus to be one of the twelve! Yet he still did not believe until later when Jesus visited again.

John 20:27-2; "*Then he said to Thomas, 'Put your finger here; see my hands. Reach out your hand and put it into my side. Stop doubting and believe.' Thomas said to him, 'My Lord and my God!' Then Jesus told him, "Because you have seen me, you have believed; blessed are those who have not seen and yet have believed."*

Let's humble ourselves and posture ourselves under God's understanding. Although we may have been through numerous experiences and have the knowledge of the world at our fingertips, that doesn't mean we know everything. Doesn't mean we are ever done being shown the lessons that are in front of us.

What haven't you given to God yet?

When's the last time I cleared my mask?

How will I place my confidence in God through the unpredictable?

Chapter 5

You cannot find Heaven by looking at everything else

Moving toward the Surface

We are all moving around in this big ocean called life. And within this ocean we all have dreams of getting to the top, to the surface of what our purpose is. Where we feel our dreams are. Just waiting for us. And there in the sandy bottom of our reality, we are contemplating constantly how to get to the "top." What we will do once we hit the pinnacle of what we deem success is. When diving, the ascent is just as important as the descent. Understanding your depth and what events need to occur before you rise to the wavy surface. First, we need to understand our depth. We need to understand how far down we have traveled and may need to make what is called a safety stop. Without this safety stop, you can be in a world of pain.

Anytime you go below thirty-three feet, it is important that on the way up you stop your ascent at between twenty and fifteen feet to prevent decompression sickness, or the "bends." While breathing the compressed air underwater, nitrogen gets accumulated in our blood.

The nitrogen then gradually gets absorbed into the tissues as the dive continues. As we start to ascend, nitrogen starts getting dispersed from the tissues as a result of decreasing the pressure of air on the tissue. However, ascending too fast will reduce the pressure very rapidly and nitrogen will try to get washed quickly. Therefore, there will be a greater pressure differential, which will cause nitrogen bubble formation in the tissues and blood vessels. These nitrogen bubbles trapped in our body will result in Decompression Sickness."[1] This is bad juju. This is noticeable on the boat if someone begins to curl their body up lying down or sitting down. The limbs will gradually move inward or bend toward the center. They will need immediate oxygen and medical assistance.

Why bring this up? A lot of believers, especially newer Christians, will have a fire for God and after a year goes by it becomes quickly extinguished because the honeymoon phase is over. There are times where people leave churches because they were never rooted and the church was merely a facility that provided encouragement from week to week. They are never really rooted in the word themselves. This is DANGEROUS. For both long-time believers and new believers, it is important to understand the longer swim to the surface, to heaven. It is important to accomplish the safety stops" fellowshipping, mentorship, Bible study, worship, small groups, and prayer. Those that do not take the time to conduct the fundamental elements of bridging a relationship with God will be like the diver in the boat that went too fast and suffered as a result. The devil will use any tactic against you. Being overzealous without seeing the bigger picture or understanding the timing of your vigor can be worked as a disadvantage. It is important to understand patience and use the appropriate methodology at certain times in our lives to maintain and build better relationships with God.

---

1 Torben Lonne, "Do Scuba Divers Really Need A Safety Stop?," last modified January 29, 2020, accessed May 1, 2020, https://www.divein.com/guide/safety-stop-why-do-i-need-to-do-it/.

Most people do not get married after knowing someone for one day. The relationship takes time to build, grow, and become familiar with one another's attitudes, behaviors, and philosophies. Likewise, it takes time to develop a relationship with God. The benefit to this relationship is that God already knows you. But to know Him takes daily effort. There are things God will only show in time.

Now let's look at the inverse, taking the safety stop. On shallow dives such as anything under forty feet, it is not necessary to complete these stops. But for deep dives it is absolutely critical. So, you make the stop, you sit at fifteen feet looking at your dive computer to complete the recommended wait time. And although you do not see the nitrogen disperse from our bodies, you know that it is happening. Just because we do not see God always working in our lives, it doesn't mean that is case. We make safety stops for a reason. A great reason. There is a dire consequence to not following recommended protocol. What do you think the dire consequences could be when we don't wait on God? When we go do our own thing? When we shift our faith from what God plans on doing to our own agenda? There are times we are called on to wait on God, to follow His direction for the betterment of our lives and to where He has called us. Remember God's timing should not be confused with our own. And this is important to remember because we are putting ourselves ahead of the processes. God has a dive plan for each and every one of us, but when we divert from the plan, we can put ourselves and others in dangerous situations with outcomes that you cannot always recover from. What does the Bible say?

- Abraham had to wait on a Son; Genesis 21:1

- Jacob waited to marry Rachel; Genesis 29:1-30

- Joseph waited in prison for his calling to be fulfilled; Genesis Chapters 37-41

- Moses and Joshua waited in the wilderness in getting to the Promise land; *Books Exodus-Joshua*
- Job waited through pain and suffering; *Book of Job*
- Daniel waited through prayer for a breakthrough; *Daniel 9*
- Mary had to believe in the promise the Angel gave in the birth of Jesus; Luke 1:26-45

Jesus's ministry was all about timing. Up to beginning His three-year ministry, His crucifixion, and now awaiting on the Father to institute the appointed the time of Him coming back.

These stories and others should reassure us that we all have times of waiting for what God wishes to fulfill in us. It's not easy all the time, it's not always convenient, but it is fulfilling. I would rather wait five to ten minutes at fifteen feet, get out, and be able to reflect on a wonderful dive experience, than get out of the water, receive CPR from a stranger, and be medevacked to the nearest hospital—all because I felt I wanted to do things my way. God's way brings about abundance and fulfillment. The Greek word for fulfilled is "pleroo." It means to make full. To fill. To abound or supply liberally. This means to give in generous amounts. I am sure that we all want to be given to in generous amounts in some part of our lives. Whether it's in our careers, finances, ventures, interests, earthly relationships, or our spiritual relationship with the Father, those things can abound in accordance to His will. It all circles back to Him and our will to sacrifice our wants to what He wants. His timing. Our timing. His way. Our way. And the outcomes become clear once a decision is made. Once your faith is fixed. Fixed on the Father or fixed on self.

Be patient. Do not confuse patience with doing nothing. Remaining active while still being obedient is a practical option. We continue to move through our faith, staying engaged while awaiting God's fullfilment. Make the most out of the safety stop—whatever that may be for you. And talk to God while you are there. Pray and worship Him. Fellowship with others. I've never been at a safety stop alone. And as a community, as a body of Christians, you are not the only one at the safety stop. Fellowship and discuss with others what you are going through. And most of all, when you get anxious or frustrated while waiting, give it to God. Allow the Holy Spirit to work while in your situation. This is the great thing about will. It's your decision. Your decision will be the igniting factor on abundance or agony. You decide whether you want to stop. In the decompression scenario, the person who shot up too quickly is the one that has to deal with being medevacked to the hospital, not anyone else. Just as the person who waited gets to receive all the benefits and memories of completing a successful dive. It's risk versus reward. In a lifetime of spiritual war that competes for your livelihood in eternal hell or eternal heaven, is the short-term risk worth jeopardizing your eternal soul?

The Dangers of Not Looking Up

Another essential element for rising to the surface while scuba diving is actually looking up. It sounds elementary, but you would be surprised by how many people do not actually look up when they are ascending. One main reason is the actual scuba vest. It is what helps you rise and sink in the water because you as the diver have the ability to inflate or deflate the vest to control your rise and fall. So people tend to fill their vest with air and start shooting their way to the surface. But outside of the decompression sickness there are many other things that are bad about quick ascents without first looking up.

This first one sounds funny, but…you could crash into wildlife! You could swim into a turtle, sting ray, other large fish, or, worse, a jellyfish. Not only will you mess up the jellyfish's day, but a face full of stingers isn't the best way to end a diving trip. You could smack into coral that is sticking out and damage the ecosystem. Or even worse, you might smack into some fire coral. Fun fact, fire coral is not actually coral but looks like it or seaweed. This coral packs a sting! They are considered Hydrozoa which is more related to jellyfish and stinging anemones! This sting that can leave you with a good rash or swelling. Interestingly enough if you are adventurous enough to dive the Jesus of the Abyss site in Florida, you will see that the statue is covered in fire coral!

By not looking up to the surface, you will inevitably hit floating debris, boat lines or anchor lines, buoys, or even the boat. You can begin to see the importance of not just knowing where you are going, but looking where you are going. Another possibility is missing the mark. You may know you're going to the surface but be yards away from your intended ascent location, i.e. the boat you rode in on. So you could be leaps and bounds away from your ride back.

For all these reasons, it is vital to look up when ascending from any dive. Now, what does this teach us about faith? We know we want to go to God, but are we actually going to Him? Here's what God showed me: we tend to focus on the things surrounding God or our lives, not focusing on Him. For those in ministry it could be the facility, the people in the church, the choir, the band, the calendar, the meetings, the routine, the money, counseling, social dynamics, attendance, and much more. And although those things serve a purpose, they are not the main purpose of the why behind it all, which is Christ. For every one of us it could be family, friends, serving the community, philanthropy, missions, careers, money, relationships, sports, education, and so much more. There are many things in our lives that God can show His presence in and through, but they are not the ultimate direction. Spending eternity with God in heaven is. Becoming distracted with elements God has given us in life is not God himself. He should be the focal point. The epicenter. As we swim in our faith, we should always be ascending towards Him and looking up. Being cognizant of what's around and every beautiful thing God shows us but seeking the surface where God resides as we move about the oceans of life remaining in the faith that keeps us from drowning.

I spoke of briefly missing the mark. It would be extremely disappointing to get to the end of life and realize that the mark has been missed. That we surface at the crossroads between Heaven and Hell to find out the boat has left us. That the Kingdom is not there waiting for us because we were not focused on the true priority. By becoming distracted, or less focused in the water, we are subject to the dangers and hazards mentioned earlier in the text. The same is true in faith. The dangers of mental health, emotional wellness, physical health, and spiritual well-being, can all become victimized by lack of attention. Having a focused purpose is essential to the elevation within your relationship with God. Not being focused can lead us down roads and paths that can cause great detriment to who we are and the gifts that we possess given by God. And the lack of fulfillment of those gifts.

Romans 12:3-8; *For by the grace given me I say to every one of you: Do not think of yourself more highly than you ought, but rather think of yourself with sober judgment, in accordance with the faith God has distributed to each of you. For just as each of us has one body with many members, and these members do not all have the same function, so in Christ we, though many, form one body, and each member belongs to all the others.*

We have different gifts, according to the grace given to each of us. If your gift is prophesying, then prophesy in accordance with your faith; if it is serving, then serve; if it is teaching, then teach; if it is to encourage, then give encouragement; if it is giving, then give generously; if it is to lead, do it diligently; if it is to show mercy, do it cheerfully.

Keep your eye on the prize and your head up. Which in all cases, scenarios, situations is always God. And He will guide you towards the ascent to which you have been called.

Boynton diving across Nine-Foot Stake Reef in Key West, Florida

No Air Scenario

Imagine you are deep in the ocean, having a good time, exploring the world around you, when all of a sudden you go to take a breath but there's no oxygen. There is no air for you to breathe in. So, naturally, it is easy to panic, eyes get big behind the mask, lose focus, and send you into a frenzy, clinging to the life itself, looking to hold and maintain the oxygen you have left, praying you make it to the surface in time. This is called a "No Air" scenario. Anytime you have an event where you run out of air in the tank, leak air, equipment malfunction, or an episode occurs that jeopardizes your air intake, is a *no bueno* situation. Diving, if you are doing it safely, is usually always a two or more-person sport due to the unpredictability of events that can take place. Everything you are taught is with a "buddy." When you are in a no air scenario, you immediately straighten your arm parallel to the ground and move it back and forth across your neck to signal your buddy you are out of air. Because obviously you can't vocalize it when under the water. Then your buddy will grab your forearm, pull you close, provide their backup respirator for you, and finally escort you to the surface. Once to the surface, your buddy will hold you up as you blow air into your BCD vest until you are buoyant. Simple! Right?

How many of us try to brave it alone? Be truthful. How many of us have been the lone ranger, the lone wolf, the lonely scuba diver? I will be the first to raise my hand. Problem with that is that it's extremely dangerous. The risks insurmountably increase against your favor when something goes bad. When we become tied up, struggling, trapped at the bottom of the waters, there is no one there to assist us. There is no one there to provide the air we need to continue our swimming journey. We use up all the air in our tanks, burn out, there's no more PSI in the tank, and we lose life that has been given to us. Sound familiar? If not, then good. If so, then welcome to party. A lot of us have been there and been the sole captain to go down with the ship. But it doesn't have to be that way. Captain America had the Avengers, Superman had the Justice League, and Jesus had the twelve disciples. Even when the disciples went out to preach, they went in twos. Fellowship is important! Fellowship with other Christians, or other believers, strengthens our faith, pushes us to continue forward, bridges gaps in perspectives, and lends new vantage points.

OK, so what does the Bible say about fellowship? The Greek word for fellowship is koinonia. Koinonia is a dynamic relationship between God and believers in their life of Christ. It describes interactive participation within the Christian community. We all belong to various communities: sports, military, career professionals, educators, parents, ethnic groups, fitness, gamers, technology enthusiasts, politicians, and the list goes on forever. And whether we play minor or major roles in these communities, we actively join with others that share the same interests. We collaborate to make the community better. And the same is with Christians. We should fellowship because of our shared adoption into Christ. We all have something in common and hope to share that love with not just each other but the world. I love watching the CrossFit games every year. I love the competition, I love how hungry the competitors are to get to the next event, and I like how positive people are that travel from all over the world to possibly win a medal on the big stage! Although I am not an avid Cross Fitter, I admire the spirit behind the greater conglomerate always pushing the community to the next level.

They want safe, clean competitions and hold competitors accountable for using illegal substances. But have you ever met a "real" Cross Fitter? My wife used to be one of them. They can never stop talking about it. They are obsessed and want to tell the entire world about their experience! And that's not a bad thing. But as we talk about our interactive fellowship in Christ…are we as passionate about Christ as the other communities that we belong to? Paul talks about this through the epistles to encourage and build each other up because we are one body. Just as I love to share and encourage others to scuba dive, I am also adamant about joining together in Christ. Why? Because I have felt what it's like going through life with "no air." Just gasping along, hoping to get to the next tank, the next competition, the next award, the next level, the next challenge. But whenever I scaled the walls, the high never lasted and I was suddenly looking for air again. As I knew God, He not only provided the air I needed going forward but put me around people who always had air in their tanks as well, people He filled. Those of us who have air in our tanks can actually focus on the daily dives and not just trying to survive. We want to thrive daily.

Are you controlling your tank, or is God?

Chapter 6

An explorer would never chart without a compass. Why as Christians would we chart the world without God?

Know Your Lifeline

On the third dive we had to be able to take off all our equipment on top of the water as well as take out the weights in the BCD (Buoyancy Control Device) vest. So we jumped into the three-foot waves and there we were just floating on top of the salty water like toys in a gigantic bathtub. This was the time for truth. To take off the very thing that was keeping me afloat in the sloshy, unruly water where I could not see anything around me or below me except the occasional jellyfish. So here we go! I had deflated all the air in my vest to get it off comfortably, unclipping all the harnesses that were strapped to me. I took the sixteen pounds of weights out, and as soon as I did, I sunk further down into the deep, dark-green water and felt more vulnerable to the unsuspecting elements and wildlife! Although I was holding onto everything I needed, I still felt unprotected. But staying focused on the task, remembering my pool training, I straddled my dive tank, which could easily keep me afloat above the water. The next step was to lie fully back onto the tank and to slide my arms back into the vest of the BCD. I clipped all my harnesses back in place around my body and put all my weights back securely in the vest.

This scenario is a very practical one, I believe. Life has a tendency to hit us with waves, uncertain and unpredictable circumstances where we may for some reason feel that we are separated from God, our lifeline. Or we take off our lifeline ourselves because we do our own thing, not realizing the depths that we are in. When we do take off the security that God provides, we become frazzled and disoriented, hoping to cling on to God as we begin to sink into the unknown variables that surround us. Just as it was important to remember my training and understand my equipment, it is important to know how God will keep us above water as my scuba tank did. When we feel separated or separate ourselves, it is important that we know that God is there, floating, waiting for us to connect. Waiting for us to use everything we have within our power to be linked and tied to all that He is. Each one of those harnesses secured me to my lifeline. The Bible, church, holy spirit, prayer, fellowshipping with others. God gives us the tools to be connected to Him. The tools are available to float above the chaos. You just have to remain latched onto Him to push through and get through.

2 Corinthians 11:23-31

I have worked much harder, been in prison more frequently, been flogged more severely, and been exposed to death again and again. Five times I received from the Jews the forty lashes minus one. Three times I was beaten with rods, once I was pelted with stones, three times I was shipwrecked, I spent a night and a day in the open sea, I have been constantly on the move. I have been in danger from rivers, in danger from bandits, in danger from my fellow Jews, in danger from Gentiles; in danger in the city, in danger in the country, in danger at sea; and in danger from false believers. I have labored and toiled and have often gone without sleep; I have known hunger and thirst and have often gone without food; I have been cold and naked. Besides everything else, I face daily the pressure of my concern for all the churches. Who is weak, and I do not feel weak? Who is led into sin, and I do not inwardly burn?

If I must boast, I will boast of the things that show my weakness. The God and Father of the Lord Jesus, who is to be praised forever, knows that I am not lying.

Unseen but Felt

There I was, swimming and floating through a world that was foreign, unconnected, and unseen by most. I was eagerly swimming on the heels of the instructor much like a baby chick on a mother hen. With every kick I could hear my breathing through the respirators. It is amazing what the unknown will do to your survival instincts. Because I was unfamiliar with the terrain, I naturally stayed very close to my instructor. If he rose, I rose. If he sank towards the sand, I was right there. When we become worried, fearful, or less confident, we lose focus and can miss some of life's most beautiful moments because we're worrying about a situation that is out of our control. When this happens, I slow my thinking down and remind myself God is in control. I remember taking in the views of the coral gullies we navigated through: bush coral, fire coral, stag horn coral, leaf coral, and large brain coral, which was the most interesting to me.

Sully coming out of a corridor on the Vandenberg Wreck dive in Key West, Florida

We soon came to the end of the one of the coral trenches. We came to an embankment (one of many that led to other paths) that we swam over.

The instructor turned around and gave me the turnaround sign so that we could head a different direction. I went behind him and turned around while the others just turned around where they were idling in the water. After about seven seconds I saw my team begin to get farther away. I was swimming, but I wasn't moving! It felt like something was holding me in place, but when I looked behind me there was nothing there. I still felt the tug of this invisible force and realized the second half of my body was inside a current! Meanwhile my team was gliding away. In the first day of training they teach you not to bicycle your legs when you swim but to straighten your legs for elongated kicks. So, I took a deep breath, relaxed, and straightened out my legs. With a little bit of effort, I jettisoned out of the current and was able to catch up with the group. I must have been in the under-water current for at least thirty seconds—thirty seconds that felt like a longer period of time. I was taken off guard, frightened for a second, and totally thrown off my game.

Life hits us with underwater currents sometimes. Things happen that are unexpected and unforeseen. But God gives us the tools to deal with these instances. We can feel we are constantly driving ourselves to move forward, but it still seems like we are in the same spot. Or caught up, sucked in the current, unable to escape. But we can escape with effort and faith to pull us out. Remember, I got out of the stream by relaxing, recalling my training, and remaining resolute. When we are blindsided by problems or situations, it is our faith that keeps us resolute in getting past the dilemma. The training equates to the time you spend with God in His word, studying, prayer, and time spent with other believers. Drawing from the word or others' experiences can be force multipliers in your success to get past a mountain that's right in front of you. Your ability to be aware, calm, and focused takes time and practice. And even then, we all, no matter the age, can be taken for a loop or two. Many say mind over matter. I get that within certain contexts, but it's really Christ over the cause that enables us not to just get through it but develop a keen sense of how God conquers all in our lives.

Whatever currents you are stuck in, remember to relax by putting the situation in God's hands, recall what God's word speaks about the situation you're going through, and allow your efforts to remain resolute in faith.

- *Abraham sacrificing his son*
- *David being chased and hunted by King Saul*
- *Joshua having to conquer Kingdoms*
- *The disciples' mentorship under Jesus*
- *Paul and his travels to across multiple cities*

These are a few snapshots from the Bible, but all faced multiple unforeseen circumstances that they had to remain faithful through. And all of them once on the other side were better and more mature in their relationship with God.

Sea Navigation

In dive four we had our last round of dive skills to demonstrate during the dive. One of the skills was compass navigation under the water. I was already sort of weary since I never really used a magnetic compass before and now, I was going to be using it underwater to not only find my way around but also help me pass the scuba diving course! Needless to say, I was a little nervous. When we arrived at the second spot for the fourth dive, I quickly put all my gear on, did our buddy checks, and proceeded to the edge of the boat. I stepped down a step onto the ladder looking at the stormy horizon through my goggles. I took the large step, splashed into the greenish grey three-foot waves, popped up and gave the master diver the okay sign.

We descended quickly down to the sand at thirty feet surrounded by the walls of coral and wildlife. As we swam a little way away from the boat, my mind was focused on the first task of underwater compass navigation, swimming, and hearing each one of my breaths through the regulator. After five minutes I found a sandy patch area where the instructor paired us up to perform the underwater compass navigation. He demonstrated what was explained in the dive plan when we were on the boat earlier. We would partner up, set our reference points based on magnetic north, and keep our lubber line straight (the lubber line or lines are the red lines on the compass). We were to swim ten kicks the direction the instructor picks, then our buddy would tell us when to stop, and finally turn around to where we started. The instructor then took out what looked like an oversized silver metal reel that would be attached to a gigantic fishing pole (This reel is used for diving on deep ship wrecks. It is called a "tagline" for divers to find their way back safely). He grooved it into the sand and pointed out directions.

Now, normally I am good with direction, but the visibility today was about ten to twelve feet horizontally, meaning I could not see past twelve feet in front of me. After about ten kicks in one direction, things would disappear. And that was exactly what happened. As the instructor pointed out my direction, I kneeled in the cold sand, set my marks, my lubber line directly straight ahead, and swam forward. When it came time to turn around, it was the moment of truth. I could no longer see where we came from. As I swam the ten kicks back my compass started moving a little wonky about five kicks in. We arrived in the same area but the wreck reel was off to my right.

The instructor had me repeat the drill! This wasn't discouraging to me but motivating, not only to get it right, but another chance to master basic underwater navigation in low visibility was exciting but nerve-wrecking at the same time. So again, I knelt into the sand, quieting my mind as I set my reference points on my compass. The instructor pointed a direction, and off I went into the blurry waters and over the beautiful corals around me. I had gotten ten kicks away and turned around immediately, moving with confidence this time. Swimming back, I almost immediately got the same issue with my compass directions going all over the place but as I straightened out the compass everything was falling into place. Suddenly my buddy tapped onto my tank and confirmed we made it back to where we started, and there was the wreck line buried into the sandy-bottom ocean floor. I looked up at the instructor, and he signaled the approval. I had passed my underwater basic navigation portion of the training.

Navigating underwater can feel a lot like navigating the world. We are taught and preached to spread the gospel among the planet, and life will take us in many directions. The beauty of this is that we should always set our reference marks on God. We should always center ourselves on God. Our "lubber lines" should always get us back to where we should start daily, which is God. God is that "wreck reel" in the sand. He is our lifeboat that is always anchored for us to swim back to. He will never leave. But at times we tend to drift and even swim away from His presence, good, bad, or indifferent. We become disconnected, like I was when I swam kicks away from the reel. There are times in our lives that we feel totally separated from where God is at. What is so amazing is that we have our compasses with us that can guide us back to where we need to be. What do I mean? Well, in this scenario, I had a buddy. The buddy represents our fellowship within the body of Christ. Mentors, Pastors, leaders, peers, or those we share our faith with in celebrating and growing in God. The compass acts as two things: The Holy Spirit who is at work in all of us offering a guiding hand, and the word. Being dialed into the word, meditating, reading, listening, gives us the opportunity to be led back to where we need to be with God. With everything that is occurring today and the daily unique challenges that we all face, the "visibility" can seem low and the world can be daunting to navigate. But using what are the tools that have been given to us freely, we can always find our way back to the anchor that God is in our lives.

Here's the thing. Are you not centered on Christ, centered on something that is fleeting, centered on things that will ultimately fade away and dissipate? Let's be honest, a lot of people center on "things" that will ultimately not last and whose tenure only is as long as whatever phase you are in life—I've done this myself in the past. People do this with sports, movies, video games, addictions to various substances, porn, technology, relationships, family members, friends, mentors, and the list can continue. I used the word anchor specifically, because it is static and when we lock in on God, that is an eternal mindset.

God lives eternally outside of the framework of time. "Jesus Christ is the same yesterday and today and forever (Hebrews 13:8).

God is the most consistent force in the universe. When we place our faith or perspectives in things that decay, change, move, or are inconsistent, we have inconsistency in our lives. It's hard to know what direction you are going when your starting point is always moving or you are always creating a new one. It is impossible to know how far left or right you are with no center focus. Life is hard to navigate with no reference point to look to. It would be like jumping off a boat into the middle of the ocean and then later trying to a find a boat that was never anchored to begin with. No man's land is where you'll be, and that's where a lot of people find themselves. Their compass is spinning in all directions because they never set their reference marks on God.

Are you moving without God's direction? In the scenario I described above I waited on the instructor to point me in the direction to swim. Have you been going in your direction and frustrated because things are not panning out? We have to trust in God that direction He reveals is the best for our lives. I did not know the reef, I was not familiar with the environment, but I didn't choose my own direction. The impressive, extraordinary, and remarkable thing is once God sends you in a direction, He has already laid everything that is needed for you without you even seeing it yet! That is why it is called faith. But His being forever omnipresent and omnipotent lends all things working in tandem in your life when you swim in the lane He has called you too. Nothing fails when God's hand is on it and those who get to know Him are never lost; "He guides me along the right paths for his name's sake" (Psalm 23:3).

- *Set your reference marks on God*

- *Take the time to center your life around Him*

- *Make the decision to allow God to point which direction your life takes*

- *You may be surprised but never lost*

Take a look around, are you centered around temporary things or people?

Your Dive Flag

The very last assessment I had was raising a dive flag from underwater. Now, a dive flag is usually an actual red flag with a diagonal white strip through the center of it that sits on a boat. It can be attached to a floatation device attached to a diver, or it can be a long-inflated bright neon colored tube that sits at the surface. Whatever the case, the flag is meant for the safety and general known location of the diver. It is an obvious symbol to all those around to stay 200 yards or more away from this area because there is a diver present. This is so the diver is to be shielded from fishing boats, jet skis, or other sea-going activities that may be going on in the area.

What we had to do at the bottom of the reef was attach a weight to the deflated dive flag; in this case it was dive line wrapped around what looked like a large fishing reel. Then once anchored to the bottom securely, we had to take out our respirators and inflate the flag with our breath a quarter of the way and then take another breath to inflate the flag the rest of the way. Everything was simple about this process except blowing into the dive flag because of the little black nasal that you had to blow into. The first time I tried, no air was going into the inflatable flag. It just sat there limp and waving in the current. The second time I tried, I was successful in getting air into the flag but put too much in initially. This was a weird experience overall due to the fact of actually holding your breath and then blowing into another source. Another thing I remember is that you should be conscientious of holding onto the dive flag because depending on your buoyancy, the dive flag can actually make you ascend as you are putting air into the flag. The best-case scenario is to blow into the flag and let it ascend while you stay below. I passed my last assessment nonetheless and rose to the surface to see the bright neon-orange flag and sun to greet me. I swam over to the boat's ladder, took off my fins in the water, handed my fins to the master diver onboard, and as I climbed the ladder, he gave me a lift up and said, "Congratulations, my friend, you are now a diver."

Like I said earlier, dive flags are important for situational awareness but even more important is your dive flag. Our ability to raise our dive flag let's all those around us know that we walk with Christ. Our lives and actions are our dive flags each day. The thing is, have you raised your dive flag or are you just another diver in the world? Does what you do represent Jesus on a daily basis?

2 Corinthians 5:20-21 NIV; *We are therefore Christ's ambassadors, as though God were making his appeal through us. We implore you on Christ's behalf: Be reconciled to God. God made him who had no sin to be sin for us, so that in him we might become the righteousness of God*

Ephesians 5:1-2 NKJV; *Therefore, be imitators of God as dear children. 2 And walk in love, as Christ also has loved us and given Himself for us, an offering and a sacrifice to God for a sweet-smelling aroma.*

Galatians 2:20 NIV; *I have been crucified with Christ; it is no longer I who live, but Christ lives in me; and the life which I now live in the flesh I live by faith in the Son of God, who loved me and gave Himself for me.*

As Christ was a representation for us, we shall be a representation for others. I mentioned earlier that before I took the steps of inflating my dive flag, I had to anchor it. As so we should be rooted in Christ. This is very important to mention. New Christians become on fire for Christ and they burn out. Similarly, long-time (lukewarm) believers can be caught in undulation because they are not anchored securely in God. So, they raise their dive flag for Christ and as significant time goes by, as a strong current, a storm, large waves come into life and their dive flag floats away, becomes damaged and unsalvageable. Why? They were never anchored fully in Christ.

Matthew 13:39; A farmer went out to sow his seed. As he was scattering the seed, some fell along the path, and the birds came and ate it up. Some fell on rocky places, where it did not have much soil. It sprang up quickly, because the soil was shallow. But when the sun came up, the plants were scorched, and they withered because they had no root. Other seed fell among thorns, which grew up and choked the plants. Still other seed fell on good soil, where it produced a crop—a hundred, sixty or thirty times what was sown. Whoever has ears, let them hear.

Matthew 13:18-23; Listen then to what the parable of the sower means: When anyone hears the message about the Kingdom and does not understand it, the evil one comes and snatches away what was sown in their heart. This is the seed sown along the path. The seed falling on rocky ground refers to someone who hears the word and at once receives it with joy. But since they have no root, they last only a short time. When trouble or persecution comes because of the word, they quickly fall away. The seed falling among the thorns refers to someone who hears the word, but the worries of this life and the deceitfulness of wealth choke the word, making it unfruitful. But the seed falling on good soil refers to someone who hears the word and understands it. This is the one who produces a crop, yielding a hundred, sixty or thirty times what was sown.

It takes effort to raise your dive flag. I'm not one to ignore the uncomfortable position someone may feel, fully accepting being a Christian in a time where being a believer in Christ can be very controversial in cultures and social circles around the world. The path we choose to walk is one that is separate from the world while still living within it. The things that gratify us are even more accessible in this modern age and flooded through all communicative means, putting added pressure on the call we have on our lives to follow, suffer, endure, and perservere for the Kingdom of God. Paul, Peter, and Jesus speak about this:

Romans 8:17; *Now if we are children, then we are heirs—heirs of God and co-heirs with Christ, if indeed we share in his sufferings in order that we may also share in his glory.*

1 Peter 3:13-15; *Who is going to harm you if you are eager to do good? But even if you should suffer for what is right, you are blessed. "Do not fear their threats; do not be frightened." But in your hearts revere Christ as Lord.*

Matthew 5:11; *Blessed are you when people insult you and persecute you, and falsely say all kinds of evil against you because of Me.*

Just as I struggled initially to blow into the small black knob that would enable my dive flag to blow up, we all have our struggles that we battle. I encourage you to continue in your efforts to dive deeper into the Bible, dive deeper into not just relationships with Christians but enhance all relationships that are in your life, and create a better dialogue with God through prayer and meditation. Perseverance is the branch to the promises of God. Every time you move forward through pain, uncomfortable situations, addiction, failure, adversity, or even the great turnouts in your life, they are a pledge, a testimony of glory God established through you. Your will to march on in faith greater inflates your dive flag for others to see. It beams to let the world around you see the light that God has placed within you. It is a further magnification of who He is and can be for those who do not know Him.

Chapter 7

Recycling didn't begin in the seventies, but when God spoke life into existence.

Abundance & Bareness

A multitude of fish and wildlife live on the Florida reef. The Florida reef is the third largest reef on the planet! It is home to over 1400 species of plants and animals. Over forty species of coral and over 500 species of fish reside there. In other words, it is a place of abundance that is swarming with life. There is an interesting feature of these reefs that I find fascinating every time that I have the opportunity to dive them. All reefs are different and they take on many shapes and forms. As you make your way around and through the reef, you are astonished by complex ecosystems that God has created with its many colors, shapes, designs, and variety of life. Conversely, you always know when you are swimming in the wrong direction off the reef (at least in the keys), because there is an apparent change in environment. The life goes away, there is no more coral, there is scarcely any fish, and the terrain becomes eerily barren. Nothing but broken shell sand and the spooky quietness. The water becomes cooler, and you have a view into a deep blue void. It is a stark contrast from before.

This is intriguing because our lives can look a lot like this before we invite Christ into our lives or when we drift too far away. My life was much like this before my faith, my belief, my trust became fully submerged in God. This does not mean that things were not going well in my life based on the way society, or the world, views success but I was not living in abundance. There was always a sense of incompleteness even when I had accomplished what were deemed amazing feats. It got to the point that I knew that things needed to change, I knew I needed a change of heart, and the accountability went past just looking in the mirror. There is a difference between moving through life and living a full meaningful life. There is a difference between just swimming about in the abyss of the ocean amongst crushed coral sands and moving to a place that is bristling with movement, growth, and sustenance. We go from a place of surviving to thriving.

The reef itself is an ecosystem that recycles itself over and over again, sustaining and perpetuating life. When God is in our lives, He becomes a well that never runs dry for our spirits. There is a perpetuating cycle of giving. The more I give myself to Him, the more I receive back in the ways I need it most. Ways that build me up in a healthy sense that I may not have even thought about before. However, it is a result of putting myself in the arms of His providence. Letting go of where I feel I need to go, and go towards Him to put me in the right place.

Hebrews 11:6; *And without faith it is impossible to please him, for whoever would draw near to God must believe that he exists and that he rewards those who seek him.*

Psalms 81:10; *I am the LORD your God, who brought you up out of the land of Egypt. Open your mouth wide, and I will fill it.*

Matthew. 6:33; *But seek first the Kingdom of God and his righteousness, and all these things will be added to you.*

"Seek" is a key term. Faith involves seeking. We often want the things that look good but fall short when we do not take the action in walking towards it. Seeking is a longing, a desire, a zeal to obtain. It is one thing to say we have faith and it is another to seek continually. To hunger for what God has in store for us.

John 14:13-14; *Whatever you ask in my name, this I will do, that the Father may be glorified in the Son. If you ask me anything in my name, I will do it.*

2 Corinthians 9:8; *And God is able to make all grace abound to you, so that having all sufficiency in all things at all times, you may abound in every good work.*

Psalm 107:9; *For he satisfies the thirsty and fills the hungry with good things.*

I challenge you to challenge what is being recycled daily in your life, circumstances and people that are not adding abundance in your life. I encourage and implore you to pray for God's abundance. Reach out in faith, and lean on Him. If God created the entirety of the world and all in it, He can provide and point you in a direction of abundance. Pray for it in the most needed areas of your life. Then walk in that belief. If you have swum away from God's providence, finding your way back can take courage. But take heart in the fact that God will be right there with you. As you pray and seek with the entirety of your heart, God will be the guiding force through your journey back to the provision needed in your life. There are no bigger arms than those of God. And His sovereignty gives comfort

Hot and Cold

We were swimming on the reefs of Key Largo on a place called the Horseshoe. And as you might imagine, the reef itself was shaped like a horseshoe. We saw tons of beautiful tropical fish, some that were eaten by us earlier that day before the dive. Where we were, we were no deeper than twenty-eight feet and under the water no more than fifty minutes. Here's the funny thing. It was the Fourth of July weekend, so the weather in the Keys was easily in the nineties, pushing into the hundreds and humid, so the water was warm to dive in. We had no need for a wetsuit because the water was about seventy-eight degrees. Like swimming in bath water. However, we had come around a part of the reef where there was a cove or small cave that we could swim through from the inside of the horseshoe reef to the outside. We went for it. We followed our guide one by one through this and after coming out of the small cove, the temperature was noticeably colder. Like almost a fifteen-degree difference. I am not one for the cold, especially after living in Florida on and off. So I was shaking a little bit adjusting to the temperature. All the same, this is how it feels as life changes around us suddenly. We are enjoying ourselves one minute and sent into a cold zone as life shifts. Things happen, and happen very rapidly at times. Nonetheless, just because the temperature changes, does not mean God has. Just because a situation changes does not mean God has left us.

- *He didn't leave Naomi and Ruth while they we living in Moab.*
- *He never left David when he fled Absalom.*
- *He never abandoned the prophet Ezekiel when he was in exile.*
- *He never left Daniel when he was taken to Babylon.*
- *He never deserted Hagar and her son Ishmael in the desert.*
- *He never left Joseph when he was a slave and prisoner in Egypt.*

When things shift in your life, realize God has not abandoned you.

James 1:2-4; *Consider it pure joy, my brothers, when you are involved in various trials, because you know that the testing of your faith produces endurance. But you must let endurance have its full effect, so that you may be mature and complete, lacking nothing.*

We all experience the testing of faith when these things arise and catch us off guard. Although taken aback by the cold, I realize that I am still on this beautiful reef God has so meticulously created with all its color and teeming life. So, although uncomfortable, there is still the appreciation for what God is providing in that moment. And although your situation is uncomfortable, God will continually exist in the midst of your struggle, in your change, in your shock.

Barracuda Family

We traveled to what was called Minnow Reef, about a mile away, and tied up there. Our guide, Denise (not her real name), warned us that we were parked near some coral that was about six feet below the boat. I am six foot one. She told me to take an extra-large step off the tail end of the boat to not damage the coral and land in twenty-six feet of water. So I walked to the edge of the thirty-foot boat, looked past the turquoise blue waters towards the sunny cloudless horizon, and splashed into the reef. Here's the funny part. Once I gave the okay signal, I quickly submerged. And once I submerged about two feet, I realized I'd dropped in right in the middle of an entire barracuda family of ten or twelve. At that moment I was surrounded by teethy barracuda who all had their eyes on this guy. The thing about barracuda in the Keys is, although they may snap, they have lots of teeth, and they are pretty mean looking...9.9 times out of 10 they swim away once you move towards them. The reef is their own buffet line with an assortment of delicacies. Don't get me wrong, I would never grab one by the tail, but honestly the danger is relatively low. So, there I was, surrounded by ten to twelve barracuda, some snapping at me, and I made up in my mind to just swim. And the moment I moved towards the sand bottom, they all dispersed and went their way.

And that's how our faith is. When we run into unlikely situations that initially seem scary, the situation snaps at us and looks pretty ugly and mean. But faith takes us through that. Our belief in God is bigger than our situation. Like the time when Elisha was sent to be captured by the King of Aram. The king had sent a whole army to surround the city of Dothan just to capture Elisha. When Elisha's servant asked, *"Oh no, my lord! What shall we do?" the servant asked. "Don't be afraid," the prophet answered. "Those who are with us are more than those who are with them. "And Elisha prayed, "Open his eyes, Lord, so that he may see." Then the Lord opened the servant's eyes, and he looked and saw the hills full of horses and chariots of fire all around Elisha. As the enemy came down toward him, Elisha prayed to the Lord, "Strike this army with blindness." So, he struck them with blindness, as Elisha had asked-2 Kings 6:15-18.*

Unexpected things will happen, and they may look frightening. That's when we do not look at fear but look at God. When I saw the barracuda, I saw what they were, I understood the possible trouble. But I know that God has made the barracuda and has also made me. He has full dominion and sovereignty over all things and every situation. I am not saying to blindly do risky stunts or escapades but merely to find peace through the faith that comes with following Jesus Christ, understanding that He is greater in your life and is the greatest of all in the universe. When confronted by a situation, settle yourself within the sovereignty of the savior.

Faith Posture

I finally made the trip to Key Largo to dive the infamous Jesus Statue. The Jesus Statue is submerged in about twenty-five feet of water and covered in all kinds of fire coral. Fire coral stings, so it's not a good idea to actually touch the statue! Most often known as the Christ of the Abyss, it is a mold of the original that is in the Mediterranean Sea near San Fruttuso. In 1961, Italian dive equipment manufacturer Egidi Cressi commissioned the third casting from the original mold and donated it to the Underwater Society of America in 1962. On August 25, 1965, it was placed in approximately twenty-five feet of water off Key Largo, Florida on Key Largo Dry Rocks.

The reef lies approximately six miles northeast of Key Largo, Florida Keys, in what was then part of the John Pennekamp Coral Reef State Park. While the statue weighs around 400 pounds, the concrete base to which it is attached weighs about 20,000 pounds.[2] Ever since I found out about this statue, I have been super eager to get out in the water to view it! So I picked up Boynton and Henson and made the two-and-a-half-hour drive up to Key Largo, where we met up with Mr. Henson (Tobi) who is a twenty plus–year retired Marine. We had lunch and made our way to the dive shop. It was over 100 degrees outside. We got our gear and eventually got on the boat. I was anxious with excitement, I had my GoPro ready, my equipment was squared away, the day was beautiful, and this was about to be A-MAZING. We pulled up to the area of the statue and then the sky began to fall. It was the Fourth of July weekend, and every human being on the planet was out on the water and anchored near the statue. Our boat captain decided to go to the reef and circle back for the second dive. We hit the reef, back on the boat after an hour dive, and circled back. This time, to my surprise there were even more people out around where the statue was supposed to be. The Captain peeled off, and my hopes sank in tandem.

2 David Jefferis, "Christ of the Abyss Statue," Christ of the Abyss Statue | Sea Dwellers Dive Center | Key Largo, FL 33037, accessed July 2020, https://www.seadwellers.com/christ-of-the-abyss-statue.htm.

Many of us think of posture as that thing our momma got after us for at the dinner table or what your teacher told you to do in school. Do not slouch. Do not lean back in your chair sort of thing. Nevertheless, sometimes we hope for things for so long and when we don't get them it heavily tests our faith posture. Situations chip away at our faith armor and can cause weighted questions that stem from a place of emotion or short-sightedness. It heavily tests our beliefs, our resilience, and our willingness to see outside of the "now." When we are tested, it gives us the opportunity to see outside of the emotions we hold internally. That is exactly what happened here. I was sorely disappointed but once we got off the boat, and made our way back to the truck, God widened my perspective when I centered myself on Him internally and not the situation. We had a safe and beautiful time off two reefs. COVID-19 was at an all-time high, people were dying, and there were people that could not even leave the house. Here I was on the world's third-largest reef, and got to not only be out of the house, but explore the wondrous diversity that goes unseen by most. Lastly, I was reminded in my spirit that I get to see Jesus daily. Visit in the word, visit in spirit, and when paying close attention, see the blessings, I am surrounded daily by that He has given me. Things that when I look at them clear-eyed, I become humbled and overwhelmed by their existence in my life. Our faith never flees or wavers when it is attached to God instead of the situation itself. There is never an "*if* this happens" scenario because He is timelessly consistent. Instead of making God the situation, we put God over the situation. Our faith becomes superficial when we place it on hollow or temporary people, moments, environments, and situations. If our God is always the same, our faith should remain the same in Him. It should not be situational or conditional.

Photograph by Sully free diving at the Christ of the Abyss dive site in Key Largo, Florida

Chapter 8

"Professionals built the Titanic, the Ark by an amateur"—unknown

Faith in Place

There is an order or a place for everything we do. The sun sits in the center of our solar system. The Earth is 70 percent water and yet it does not wash over the masses of land that we inhabit. With my diving equipment, every piece, attachment, clip, flipper, mask, tank, reader, and tube has a specific place. The O-ring on a scuba tank is no bigger than the circumference of your pinky finger. The rubber O-ring is vitally important. It keeps all the air from seeping out and water getting in. This small rubber piece that could pass for a child's size hairtie, keeps people from running out of air while underwater. Talk about incredible. hundreds of dollars' worth of equipment rendered useless with a tiny little circular rubber piece that seems insignificant but has an important place. Similarly, when I swim below the surface and I am encountered with the jubilant colors of thousands of coral, hundreds of fish, and broken shell sands, I see that everything has a place. It has a spot that it inhabits within the ecosystem. This is very important when we look at our place, our space that we have been placed into.

Everything that I mentioned before has an intended space for a reason. God's design is flawless. And the question becomes, why is it here? Why I am here in this place at this time? I believe it is a fair question.

Our life's design it to meet God's intended purpose. That purpose is unique to the time-frames we move through moment to moment. We become so caught up on the place, we become blind in our thought process as to what God's purpose is in this specific space, we are in. Whether we are dealing with death, cumbersome relationships, incarceration, addiction, parenthood, sexuality, academic challenges, health problems, or the multitude of diverse quandaries we come across, the truth is that we are in this place. How will God's light shine through you in this place? Joseph after being thrown in jail for a crime he did not commit, while in prison, interpreted dreams for the two other prisoners. This ignited the catalyst for him to be in front of pharaoh much later (1Sam 25:1-1Sam 25:42) .Abigail was married to a drunken, evil man. A man, his servants, and all that he owned was on the brink from being snuffed out because of his criticism and insolence he discharged towards King David. But Abigail's faith and wisdom saved everyone from being destroyed, even Nabal. Her ability to be faithful to God in the "place" God had her saved people's lives.

1 Samuel 25:32-35 NKJV; Then David said to Abigail: *"Blessed is the Lord God of Israel, who sent you this day to meet me! And blessed is your advice and blessed are you, because you have kept me this day from coming to bloodshed and from avenging myself with my own hand. For indeed, as the Lord God of Israel lives, who has kept me back from hurting you, unless you had hurried and come to meet me, surely by morning light no males would have been left to Nabal!" So David received from her hand what she had brought him, and said to her, "Go up in peace to your house. See, I have heeded your voice and respected your person.*

Ten days later, Nabal died and King David then proposed to Abigail. Daniel was taken from Judah into Babylon as a young man and his faith in place enabled him over time to be the third-highest ruler in the Kingdom. But Daniel faced trials of his own. Daniel chose not to defile himself, he never stopped praying, and he continued to have faith even when it didn't reflect the views of those in authority that were not following God. Mordecai's faith as part of the captives carried away from Jerusalem—his faith that God would use Esther in a mighty way in the midst of being ripped away from all they knew. Esther after a year was selected as the queen. And when Haman plotted against Mordecai, God raised Mordecai in great favor before the king as well as using Esther as a covering over the Jews. After a twelve-month period, they went from captives to conquerors. From poor to provisioners. They had gained high favor with the most powerful man in the land and provided a covering over God's people, all because of their faith in place.

If the situation was always ideal, then we would never need faith. We would never need to lean on God's will to play out for our lives, because everything would work out perfectly. We know that this is not the world we live in. It's full of situations that come about and many without warning. Our faith in place opens opportunity for God to use us within His total sovereignty for His glory. Not only will He establish us in our place, but he will also bring to light why He is so powerful. We need to have faith in the place we are in to get us and others the places we wish to go in Him. God will never put us in a place without provision. Scope your faith around God, and He will place the appropriate provision around His children.

Hebrews 11:7; *By faith Noah, when warned about things not yet seen, in holy fear built an ark to save his family. By his faith he condemned the world and became heir of the righteousness that is in keeping with faith.*

Noah was not an expert on boats. Noah was not a fisherman or sea-going man. He was not a zoologist. He was no Dr. Doolittle (he didn't speak animal languages). The text does not say he was an expert carpenter by any means. When the text characterizes Noah, the Scripture says, "Noah was a righteous man, blameless among the people of his time, and he walked faithfully with God" (Genesis 6:9). Out of all the people in the world, the entirety of the planet, Noah walked faithfully. Where Noah was, he moved faithfully in God's sight. And because of his faith in place, God gave him a set of instructions that not only saved his family but were the only ones left after the great flood. God gave Noah directions that did not match his current situation. Noah's faith was not capsuled by circumstance.

Because he was faithful already, his faith led him to live while things around him were dying. While the world was literally drowning, Noah was lifted up. "For forty days the flood kept coming on the earth, and as the waters increased they lifted the ark high above the earth. The waters rose and increased greatly on the earth, and the ark floated on the surface of the water. They rose greatly on the earth, and all the high mountains under the entire heavens were covered" (Genesis 7:17-19). How much more would God use Noah's faith during the flood and after the flood? Noah did not know how long it was going to rain; how long would the entirety of the Earth would be filled with water? He had to have faith in place while on the water and to add the element of every animal living with him on the boat! Once the Ark made landfall, he had to be able to reestablish a living in a strange new place. A new world. Everything of old had washed away. When you are at the helm of being the only living humans on the planet, you've got to have faith in your place.

Hebrews 11:11-12; *And by faith even Sarah, who was past child-bearing age, was enabled to bear children because she considered him faithful who had made the promise. And so from this one man, and he as good as dead, came descendants as numerous as the stars in the sky and as countless as the sand on the seashore.*

Abram was eighty-six when Sarai gave over her maidservant Hagar to him that they might bare a child through her servant. Scripture says Sarai had borne Abram no children. She was past the age of delivering a child. So they attempted to have a child their own way. And this way created strong resentment between Sarai and Hagar, so much anger and bitterness that Hagar and her son Ishmael were sent away! Now the Lord appeared to Abraham when he was ninety-nine years of age and still promised a son that would be borne through Sarah.

Genesis 17:15-20

Then God said to Abraham, "As for Sarai your wife, you shall not call her name Sarai, but Sarah shall be her name. And I will bless her and also give you a son by her; then I will bless her, and she shall be a mother of nations; kings of peoples shall be from her."

Then Abraham fell on his face and laughed, and said in his heart, "Shall a child be born to a man who is one hundred years old? And shall Sarah, who is ninety years old, bear a child?" And Abraham said to God, "Oh, that Ishmael might live before You!"

Then God said: "No, Sarah your wife shall bear you a son, and you shall call his name Isaac; I will establish My covenant with him for an everlasting covenant, and with his descendants after him. And as for Ishmael,

I have heard you. Behold, I have blessed him, and will make him fruitful, and will multiply him exceedingly.

Although we see the promise of God in Chapter 17 of Genesis, we also see Abraham's disbelief. As a matter of fact, he laughs about it. Abraham was in pure disbelief. God appears again in Genesis 18, revealing himself to Abraham, and echoes the promise yet again of a son being born through Sarah at the age of 100 years. At this point Sarah scoffs at God in disbelief and laughter. As obedient as Abraham and Sarah were, they still lacked faith that God would provide the miracles that they had craved for so long. This dream seemed impossible at this stage in their lives. It is faith the looks past current into what's coming. We settle for current too much. God is always working in what's coming. It is already set into motion. We too much allow the current time to tamper with what God has already done in tomorrow. Our faith is our confidence in the future. Faith fights these fires of disbelief. God showed himself to Abraham twice. God himself gave word to Abraham. We can point fingers at Abraham all day, but the truth is that's what makes God the one of miracles and us human.

God does the things that can only be accomplished by Him. He displays why He is the sole savior of all humanity within His perfect timing. When there is no other way, the miracle, the solution can only happen when God's hand is in the mix. Sarah's womb was done. Finito by our standards. You can never close the curtain on the window God places in your life for Him to shine through. God has the final word. And it's not until Genesis 21 that we see the birth of Isaac. Faith in place is hard. God wants to do incredible miraculous acts in our lives, but our faith has to be as big as our God is. It's hard to be obedient when you are not fully faithful. To not have faith in what God has called in your life is to not believe. And the entire fundamental root of everything is belief. It is tough. No shirking around it. Abraham, the patriarch. The one that received the legendary promise:

Genesis 17:1-6 NKJV; *When Abram was ninety-nine years old, the Lord appeared to Abram and said to him, "I am Almighty God; walk before Me and be blameless. And I will make My covenant between Me and you, and will multiply you exceedingly." Then Abram fell on his face, and God talked with him, saying: "As for Me, behold, My covenant is with you, and you shall be a father of many nations. No longer shall your name be called Abram, but your name shall be Abraham; for I have made you a father of many nations. I will make you exceedingly fruitful; and I will make nations of you, and kings shall come from you.*

Abraham fought with his faith. We strive to understand, but what it comes down to for us is to just believe. And walk in that belief prayerfully daily. Move through God's promises faithfully , patiently, and resiliently. It's a challenging ask on everybody. We desire to get to the promise so expeditiously that we trip ourselves up sometimes rushing the process. Nothing is too limiting for God. He created the womb, so he can open it as He did with Sarah. He created all things and all things are submissive to His guidance. Are you submissive to God's will for your life or your own? Abraham and Sarah tried to makeshift a family, and Abraham eventually ended up watching his first son leave. Abraham had to wait fourteen years before he saw his son Isaac born! What is God having you wait for?

Hebrews 11:24-27; By faith Moses, when he had grown up, refused to be known as the son of Pharaoh's daughter. He chose to be mistreated along with the people of God rather than to enjoy the fleeting pleasures of sin. He regarded disgrace for the sake of Christ as of greater value than the treasures of Egypt, because he was looking ahead to his reward. By faith he left Egypt, not fearing the king's anger; he persevered because he saw him who is invisible.

Hebrews 11:31; By faith the prostitute Rahab, because she welcomed the spies, was not killed with those who were disobedient.

Jericho was a mighty city. A city that stood on its own. Moreover, the King of Jericho was made aware of the spies' presence that were sent by Joshua to scout the city. The King knew the spies were in Rahab's house. The King was aware of an enemy presence within his own city, their location, and whose house it was. "So the King of Jericho sent this message to Rahab: "Bring out the men who came to you and entered your house, because they have come to spy out the whole land." At this point, it seemed as though the jig was up. Cats out of the bag. It is all over but the crying. Elvis has left the building. Rahab had no loyalty to these spies. She worked in that city. She was a prostitute who most likely knew a fair percentage of the people who lived there in Jericho. Although she had hidden them in the roof, she could have easily turned over the spies to their pursuers.

She could have easily dimed them out. But later in Joshua 2 it says, "I know that the Lord has given you this land and that a great fear of you has fallen on us, so that all who live in this country are melting in fear because of you. We have heard how the Lord dried up the water of the Red Sea for you when you came out of Egypt, and what you did to Sihon and Og, the two kings of the Amorites east of the Jordan, whom you completely destroyed. When we heard of it, our hearts melted in fear and everyone's courage failed because of you, for the Lord your God is God in heaven above and on the earth below."

Her faith in God's authority and power outweighed the authorities that were there in that place of Jericho.

Hebrews 11:30; By faith the walls of Jericho fell, after the army had marched around them for seven days.

Imagine standing on the footsteps of the mighty Jericho walls as Joshua. The gates barred from the Israelites, and no one had been allowed in or out of the city. Joshua stood there with the entire nation behind him peering up at the tall walls that loomed in front of them. What most people do not know about Jericho was that there was at ground level the retaining wall that stood thirteen to fifteen feet tall. Then above and behind the retaining wall was the lower city wall that was about twenty-eight feet tall that sat on top of the embankment of earth. Then some distance back and farther up was the higher city wall that was thirteen feet tall but the wall itself sat about fifty feet above the ground level mentioned earlier. Then add on the thirty-foot watch-tower. Joshua and the Israelites walked upon one of the modern super-structures of their day, a cumulative eighty feet of defenses around the city. As well-known as Jericho was, they still barred their gates. You would think that God would have given Joshua an advanced military tactic: scaling the walls, using someone on the inside, a trojan horse, or launching fiery arrows into the city! Nope.

Joshua 6:2-5; Then the Lord said to Joshua, "See, I have delivered Jericho into your hands, along with its king and its fighting men. March around the city once with all the armed men. Do this for six days. Have seven priests carry trumpets of rams' horns in front of the ark. On the seventh day, march around the city seven times, with the priests blowing the trumpets. When you hear them sound a long blast on the trumpets, have the whole army give a loud shout; then the wall of the city will collapse and the army will go up, everyone straight in.

Joshua, I want you to simply march around the city fortress without saying a sound. They spent six days without making a sound as they marched around Jericho. That's why I am glad it was Joshua. Because pitching to your people that we are going to march in silence around the formidable Jericho doesn't seem as though it would bode over well. But the people had faith in Joshua, and Joshua in the Lord. I believe God could have asked Joshua to do the tootsie roll and he would have done it. Joshua didn't second guess God's direction. They were objectively in a scenario that on paper should have been one of the Israelites' toughest challenges. But Joshua's faith was as big as his God. Joshua didn't hesitate, he didn't question or say we'll try that later. He marched. And they walked in faith. They walked in faith until the walls came down on the seventh day as God had promised. And what a physical representation of walls that can be torn down by walking in faith. Not disputing God. Not disputing the circumstance. But just marching in your faith waiting for God's promise to be fulfilled. The Israelites didn't even have to break a brick with their bare hands. What mighty walls are you staring at, and all God is asking for you to do is march? Walk in the faith I have instilled in you. Are you allowing the look of your Jericho to overpower the reality that God wants for your life?

Henson travels through the inner spaces of the Vandenberg Wreck Key West, Florida

Chapter 9

There are opportunities only God can open.

Vandenberg

Living out in Key West has posed some pretty unique opportunities. One opportunity was initially daunting and brought extreme enthusiasm. The USNS General Hoyt S. Vandenberg is a ship that was sunken in Key West waters and sits 140 feet deep in the Atlantic Ocean. The ship is 522 feet long and weighs 17,000 tons. The Vandenberg actually belonged to the Air Force in 1961 and was used to track missiles and spacecraft launches. Interestingly enough, the ship was filmed in the movie *Virus* and is considered an artificial reef in Key West. It is the fourth most popular wreck dive on the planet. We had the fortunate opportunity to take a charter out to this magnificent dive site. Understand that this was the deepest and most advanced dive that we had accomplished up to this point. Furthermore, as a wreck dive it had its own precautionary and safety measures.

So, as we traveled towards our destination through the emerald waters, they soon turned a steel blue. This was a good indicator we were not in Kansas anymore and out of our normal dive depths. Our dive guide explicitly broke down the dive plan. We were going to jump in off the back of the boat, grab ahold of the mooring line, swim down fifteen feet, and pull ourselves across a fifty-foot line that paralleled the Navy ship. Once we got to the middle of the rope, there to the center line, we would descend down to sixty feet above a platform on the ship. Once everyone was there safely, we would descend to the deck of the Vandenberg, which would be our main piloting level of 101 feet. Because there was no current and the visibility was eighty to ninety feet clear, once we started to descend from fifteen feet, it was like free-falling all the way down to the main deck as we watched the ship get larger and larger the faster we descended. We dove the Vandenberg twice with max bottom times being seventeen minutes a tour. There were some astonishing things we saw down at those depths while exploring around and inside the US Navy vessel that were both striking and enlightening.

Out of Your Depth

At those depths, if an emergency happens it is handled at that level. You cannot just zoom to the surface because you will incur decompression sickness (which can kill you) and, depending on the emergency, you will have to rely on your team and the skills that help you survive. Our faith is the embodiment of this scenario. As we move deeper into our lives, we should put our total faith and reliance on God. I had to have faith stepping off the boat into those deep waters, leaving my physical place of surety in the boat for the greater things God had in store. I had to have faith that God would cover me within the unknown. The greater assurance lies in the great One. When we are faced with fear of unknown outcomes, we forge our faith in the

Father of our future. We can never get to the pilot levels, the depths God wants us to reach by staying in the boat or worrying about what might happen. Although the dive was advanced, God advances in front of me.

Henson & Dive Guide float towards the bridge of the Vandenberg Key West, Florida

Deuteronomy 31:8 "It is the Lord who goes before you. He will be with you; he will not leave you or forsake you. Do not fear or be dismayed."

- Moses felt out of his depth going back to Egypt to lead the Hebrews.

- Gideon felt out of his depth when he was called to fight against the Midianites, Amalekites, and other eastern peoples.

- Jonah was thrown into the depths and before dying God sent a great fish to swallow him and guide him back on the right path towards Nineveh.

- There were a couple of times within the Gospel the disciples felt out of their depth, sometimes even while they were with Jesus.

- Naomi felt out of her depth when she experienced the loss of her sons and husband.

- Daniel, Hananiah, Mishael, and Azariah were taken away from Judah to Babylon.

- Saul was confronted by Jesus on the way to Damascus.

The examples can go on, but the point is we all succumb to being out of our depths one way or another during this lifetime. What will you put your faith in once it happens? Will it be God?

God's Dive Light

The ship had the ability to carry 3,200 troops aboard, which meant there were a lot of rooms aboard the vessel. While down there, we explored the bridge and large passageways. We went into corridors and swam through areas that were lit up by the light reflecting in the ocean. We got to swim through some areas looking down into multiple decks of the interior of the ship, seeing and being mindful of the super structure and its large history. There were hollow halls covered bounteously in coral, and fish coming out of every opening. We were looking out the windows into the vast blueness. As we moved into some areas of the ship, there was no light and we had to turn on our dive lights. And I'll tell you what. There's nothing that'll stand your hairs up more than swimming down dark hallways, rooms, and elevator shafts at 100 feet below. Our lights would catch the rusted metal gelled with brittle coral and at times they would illuminate the darker, uninhabited forgotten decks where the Moray eels played. And it was fascinating to see the aggregations of fish that burrowed themselves away within the steeled darkness. But the light revealed the hidden beauty of the secret interior passageways and creatures that lurked within. Our flashlights uncloaked the life that routinely goes unseen. In the same vein, as we allow God within the deepest darkest parts of our lives, whether be it present or past, His light peers in and illuminates what seemed to be ignored or far removed. He uses the life experiences of then and now in the advancement of His glory placed in you and for others. It takes vulnerability and courage to plunge into these dark areas led by God. It takes heart to give God our heart in these circumstances.

Henson marvels within the starboard corridor
of the Vandenberg ship wreck Key West, Florida

Ezekiel 36:26; *And I will give you a new heart, and a new spirit I will put within you. And I will remove the heart of stone from your flesh and give you a heart of flesh.*

By allowing God's light in, we allow God to renew our Spirits, to renew us from the circumstances, the struggles, the sickness, the trauma, the bitterness, and the strife. To be renewed in Christ is to be restored in a way that you're built up and stronger because He is stronger.

Let's take Job for example. Job had it all. He was even considered righteous before God. That's impressive! But Job got everything wiped out of his life. His kids, his wealth, and his health. And with all that Job went through as it happens in the Bible, he was restored far greater than before.

Job 42:10; "The *Lord restored the fortunes of Job when he prayed for his friends, and the Lord gave Job twice as much as he had before.*"

But Job went through so many heavy things before it came to that point. And life presents us with heavy events, and presents us with opportunity that at times leads to the wrong choices that manifest mistakes. But when we give "it" over to God and give ourselves to Him, He will use what was broken and torn apart for a magnifying miracle. I mentioned the fish life that was hidden in those dark corridors. God brings out the beauty that resides behind those dark rooms locked away. But it all starts with an act of faith. Faith of letting in His light… say this prayer for God to break through in your life:

God, I've held somethings in my heart,

I have some things stored in my heart I want to let go of,

I want to give those things to you,

I want your spirit to continually come into my life,

Turn my struggle into your glory,

Allow who you are to be magnified in my life and help me to see you daily,

Give me your strength to move past this situation and others than I may not know of,

I praise you, I love you, I worship and thank you,
We believe that all things can be accomplished in Jesus holy name,
Amen.

Lionfish

The lionfish is one of the most prolific fish that is out there. Why? Take a look at any villain's fish tank in a movie and I'll guarantee you'll see a lionfish. You may not have known the name, but you will recognize it once you see it. The lionfish is a brown fish with white stripes and a whole lot of spines. Those venomous spines sting. And if they sting, you'll feel it for days. The venom from their spines alone can last for days, causing intense pain, respiratory issues, and paralysis. The lionfish is a blooming invasive species to reefs. They have no natural predators and they themselves are predators. They kill off helpful species to the reef and are growing. So fishers and divers alike are encouraged to kill this fish to aid in saving ecosystems. I hear they are good meals as well!

Subsequently, down at ninety feet swimming out off a shadowy corridor, I turned around with my GoPro to get my buddy Henson to get a good video shot, and my dive light happened to shine towards the balcony ceiling. And there three feet from my face was this good-sized lionfish just staring at me. And in the matter of a couple seconds, I felt nervous, I thought, "Bring it on", and then I felt at peace with the situation. He was watching me and I was watching him. And as the seconds went on, I became more and more excited to see this animal, with such as notorious reputation, from a relatively safe position to encounter this animal in its natural element on a ship wreck. It was the first one I ever saw diving, and I will never forget the experience.

There are things that could happen to us every day that we are protected from and that we are oblivious to. I literally swam two feet under that lionfish without seeing it. There could have been some consequences had I made contact with that animal. Not only was I made aware of the animal, but I was also given peace when confronted by it. I never let my emotions, information, or the possibility of harm get in the way of what I know to be true, which is that God is in control.

Lion fish found 90 feet down on the Vandenberg wreck dive Key West, Florida

David sang to the Lord the words of this song when the Lord delivered him from the hand of all his enemies and from the hand of Saul. He said:

2 Samuel 22:1-3

"The Lord is my rock, my fortress and my deliverer;

my God is my rock, in whom I take refuge,

my shield and the horn of my salvation.

He is my stronghold, my refuge and my savior—

from violent people you save me

Psalm 91:9-16

If you say, "The Lord is my refuge,"

and you make the Most High your dwelling,

no harm will overtake you,

no disaster will come near your tent.

For he will command his angels concerning you

to guard you in all your ways;

they will lift you up in their hands,

so that you will not strike your foot against a stone.

You will tread on the lion and the cobra;

you will trample the great lion and the serpent.

"Because he loves me," says the Lord, "I will rescue him;

I will protect him, for he acknowledges my name.

He will call on me, and I will answer him;

I will be with him in trouble,

I will deliver him and honor him.

With long life I will satisfy him

and show him my salvation.

Chapter 10

It's hard to notice the diamond when you see it as just a rock!

Smooth as Glass

I woke up, got ready, popped some Dramamine and started my one-mile walk to the dive shop. It was 0800 when I arrived. We checked in, got our gear over to the boat, set up the gear on our tanks, and away we went out to the deep blue ocean. This was the second time we were going to dive the USN Vandenberg, and we'd picked a beautiful day. We happened to have the Monday off due to Columbus Day. There was no wind, and the sun was beaming off the water. And on top of that there were literally no waves in the water. It looked like glass. Sailing out to the ship, we saw a pod of dolphins playing in the wake of the boat. The conditions could not have been better for this trip. We pulled up to the floating mooring balls at the ship's location, then started preparing our gear, performing our buddy checks, putting on our gloves, and strapping on our flippers. Our boat captain got to the end of the boat, looked down, and said, "Current is not looking great. Looks at least two knots."

Fun fact: the average person can only swim one knot of speed. Swimming in a two-knot current can easily whist you far away from dive lines and way out to sea. I was confused; the ocean looked flatter than a flounder flap jack. Our guide jumped in the water to check out the situation. And when she came up, she validated the Captain's prediction. It wasn't safe to be swimming down there and even if we all were advanced swimmers, the dive wouldn't have been enjoyable fighting a current the whole time. Although most were bummed out about the call, I was surely wasn't. The reward didn't outweigh the risk. I would hate to be 100 feet down in the ocean and swept away to be swallowed up into the great deep! I wouldn't even want to be swept away while at the surface of the ocean! Ironically enough, five minutes later, another boat pulled up to a separate mooring line tied to the USN Vandenberg. A guy jumped into the water and literally started whaling and panicking as the current nearly swept him away! He barley grabbed hold of the end of the line in the water after shuffling about fifteen to twenty feet and yelled out, "Y'all better grab hold of that line when you fall in! That current will take ya!" Our Captain made the decision to head to another wreck, the Cayman Salvage.

Before I get to that, let us pause for a second. What we see is not always what we get. The sea was like glass that day, but where the USN Vandenberg was, the current was strong. It was not a safe swim for the average person. What we had planned for was not what we got. We may be presented with situations that on the onset look beautiful and glassy. But underneath it all, the waters are churning and kicking, ready to pull you away. There are times God tells us and shows us to make directional shifts in our lives. I couldn't see the current until our guide got into the water and drifted fast underneath the surface. We may not always understand, but there are times when we arrive to a place and before we walk in the doors God tells us to go somewhere else. Unbeknownst to us, there is a raging current on the other side of that "door." On the other side of the "opportunity," on the other side of that relationship with that person, on the other side of that "job" in that "place." Faith is being able to get to the water and listen to the Captain. When you are on the cusp of that thing you've wanted to do, and God says no. We often look at faith as getting through something or getting to something. But faith is also moving *from* something. Even when it is what you have craved and wanted, when you are facing what you thought was your future and God says, "Come this way."

John 5:1-15

Healing at the Pool (NKJV); *After this there was a feast of the Jews, and Jesus went up to Jerusalem. Now there is in Jerusalem by the Sheep Gate a pool, which is called in Hebrew, Bethesda, having five porches. In these lay a great multitude of sick people, blind, lame, paralyzed, waiting for the moving of the water. For an angel went down at a certain time into the pool and stirred up the water; then whoever stepped in first, after the stirring of the water, was made well of whatever disease he had. Now a certain man was there who had an infirmity thirty-eight years. When Jesus saw him lying there, and knew that he already had been in that condition a long time, He said to him, "Do you want to be made well?"*

The sick man answered Him, "Sir, I have no man to put me into the pool when the water is stirred up; but while I am coming, another steps down before me."

Jesus said to him, "Rise, take up your bed and walk." And immediately the man was made well, took up his bed, and walked.

And that day was the Sabbath. The Jews therefore said to him who was cured, "It is the Sabbath; it is not lawful for you to carry your bed."

He answered them, "He who made me well said to me, 'Take up your bed and walk.'"

Then they asked him, "Who is the Man who said to you, 'Take up your bed and walk'?" But the one who was healed did not know who it was, for Jesus had withdrawn, a multitude being in that place. Afterward Jesus found him in the temple, and said to him, "See, you have been made well. Sin no more, lest a worse thing come upon you."

The man departed and told the Jews that it was Jesus who had made him well.

In this scenario, the man was so focused on the pool that he didn't even recognize that Jesus was right in front of Him. The answer was right in front of him, but who could blame this guy? He had been struggling for thirty-eight years before Jesus had come to speak with him. And this poor man had watched the water be stirred and stirred, not ever to receive the healing. Something he wanted for thirty-eight years! But when he encountered Jesus, he was empowered by Jesus and elevated. When we in our faith look at the Captain (God) despite how bad we have desired something, we open ourselves to an encounter with God. Then He empowers us to move within the accordance of His will, and finally elevates us to where we need to be. I often say our obedience is an opportunity for others. The man's testimony to all the religious leaders and people was pointing to the obedience of Christ and all that He is. Are you playing the Captain when you should just be listening as the diver?

We had never dived the Cayman Salvage Master. The Cayman Salvage was built in 1937 and when it sank down in ninety feet of water, it originally sank on its side. Thanks to Hurricane Kate, the Cayman was in recent years moved to its upright position, where it sits in now. The Cayman has done it all. From World War II, to Navy VIP ship, to Army Ship, to drug-smuggling ship, to a ship that transported over 5000 Cubans to the Florida Keys! This ship has some character. When we got into the water, there were beautiful pink jellyfish floating and about fifty feet of visibility. We pulled our way down to about seventy feet towards the bow of the ship. We swam twenty feet further down to the boat's bottom, which was surrounded by a reef that existed at ninety feet at the sand.

Dive Guide gazing into giant open well
of the Cayman Salvage Master Key West, Florida

I had never been to the sand at that depth before. There was so much silt at that level the visibility seemed chalky. Which made the water look a brownish grey. It looked like the moon and Mars. We ran into a baby lionfish within some coral, and saw barracuda and a number of other creatures. It was like being an astronaut in a fish tank. We swam up to the boat's bow and explored the eerie deck that had empty algae- and seaweed-covered stairwells that were dark and abandoned. There was also a large circular well that I had the opportunity to submerge in and with my dive light got to see an inside portion of this small vessel. At 187 feet long the boat didn't take long to traverse, but it was still an amazing opportunity to view another wreck and another part of history that lives even at the bottom of the sea. What I expected shifted and what I got a chance to see was more than I anticipated. When we allow God to change our anticipations to His expectations, we have the opportunity to receive the elevation that He has in store for us one way or another.

Sunset Key

Sully at Sunset Key West, Florida

Here I was. I'd just picked up some fresh diving equipment on my way to the Sigsbee Marina to meet my boys Henson and Tom. I had a new Hawaiian sling that I had never used in my life, and I wasn't afraid to use it. What's a Hawaiian sling? Usually, a yellow pole that is three or six feet long with a three-pronged spear resting at the top. Why the spear, you ask? Well, Henson, Tom, and I were going to Sunset Key to hunt for lionfish. I stayed up all night the night before researching the toxin of the fish, why it is OK to hunt lionfish, and watching plenty of videos of people hunting them around the world. Pumped up and nervous, we packed up Tom's dingy and made the trek out to Sunset Key from the marina. We anchored near a reef shelf and at the deepest point it was suspected to be thirty feet. Tom was there freediving; Henson and I threw on our gear as we sat on the edge of the coral shelf and popped in the water. The water visibility was five feet at best. We'd gotten a tip that lionfish were in the area, and I was pretty on edge for our safety, hoping that we saw them before they saw us.

We sank down between fifteen and twenty feet, looming over the coral wall for these notorious lionfish. It was quiet along the wall that was to my right and to my left just milky blueish green water where there was no telling what else was swimming out there. At one point a four-foot reef shark came swimming by in the shadows. Barracudas, tarpan, and whatever else that couldn't be seen clearly. And the worst the visibility the deeper we went. The sun's sparce rays of light gave us some illumination down to the sand at twenty-eight feet as the water got cooler. And after an hour of searching in the gloomy waters of Sunset Key we found no lionfish! But I will tell what we did find…the most lobster I had ever seen in my life. What started as an intense hunt for lionfish, ended up as a wonderful day of exploring the multitudes of lobster that were happy to greet us. I am not a lobster eater nor really big into seafood in general, but I am sure many people would've been ready with the butter on their plates to eat those huge suckers! The closest I've been to lobster is at the grocery store when they are floating around in the large fish tanks. There must have been dozens of lobsters hanging out, as well as, of course, parrot fish, angel fish, snapper, and horseshoe crabs.

What I set out for was not what I ended up with. God showed me a different set of creatures that made their homes with the coral shelves of the murky mangrove type waters. How often we are so disappointed by not seeing what we wanted to see. I didn't see one lionfish. But God showed me a lot more. I wonder how our perspectives would change if we didn't focus on what is not there and shift our attention to what is? Too often, we look at the absence instead of what is present. What is God currently showing you? As murky as it was in Sunset Key, God opened up an entire ecosphere of life in front of me that I never anticipated. It was like being on National Geographic, except I wasn't a scientist or world renown photographer. Right here in my own backyard, hanging out with the large tarpan, manatees, reef sharks, lobsters, and schools of fish. Curbing anticipation to see what is present, rather than what is absent—how does this fuel our faith? Grasping God's gifts, as subtle as they may be, at times further supports our faith in God. If I can see more and more of the provision God puts in my life, it further drives my understanding of how God is a provider. If I take notice of the love God has placed in my life, I can further learn from the heart of God. The major cornerstone of this point is "noticing," taking time to step back and notice the characteristics of God working around me. "But Sully, how can I notice God in my life?" That is a fair question. This is the same as asking, "How can I notice a fish If I never have seen one to be able to identify?" This is why we read the word of God (the Bible). The Bible will display God in all His attributes. Just as anyone would go to Google to research a topic, TikTok to learn a dance, or YouTube to learn from a tutorial, the Bible is where you will learn who God is and learn to connect more to what God is calling you to see that is right in front of your eyes. It's hard to notice the diamond when you see it as just a rock!

Chapter 11

Praise the Lord, my soul.

Lord my God, you are very great;
you are clothed with splendor and majesty.

The Lord wraps himself in light as with a garment;
he stretches out the heavens like a tent
and lays the beams of his upper chambers on their waters.
He makes the clouds his chariot
and rides on the wings of the wind.
He makes winds his messengers,
flames of fire his servants.

He set the earth on its foundations;
it can never be moved.
You covered it with the watery depths as with a garment;
the waters stood above the mountains.
But at your rebuke the waters fled,
at the sound of your thunder they took to flight;
they flowed over the mountains,
they went down into the valleys,
to the place you assigned for them.

You set a boundary they cannot cross;
never again will they cover the earth.

He makes springs pour water into the ravines;
it flows between the mountains.
They give water to all the beasts of the field;
the wild donkeys quench their thirst.
The birds of the sky nest by the waters;
they sing among the branches.
He waters the mountains from his upper chambers;
the land is satisfied by the fruit of his work.
He makes grass grow for the cattle,
and plants for people to cultivate—
bringing forth food from the earth:
wine that gladdens human hearts,
oil to make their faces shine,
and bread that sustains their hearts.
The trees of the Lord are well watered,
the cedars of Lebanon that he planted.
There the birds make their nests;
the stork has its home in the junipers.
The high mountains belong to the wild goats;
the crags are a refuge for the hyrax.

He made the moon to mark the seasons,
and the sun knows when to go down.
You bring darkness, it becomes night,
and all the beasts of the forest prowl.
The lions roar for their prey
and seek their food from God.
The sun rises, and they steal away;
they return and lie down in their dens.
Then people go out to their work,
to their labor until evening.

How many are your works, Lord!
In wisdom you made them all;
the earth is full of your creatures.
There is the sea, vast and spacious,
teeming with creatures beyond number—
living things both large and small.
There the ships go to and fro,
and Leviathan, which you formed to frolic there.

All creatures look to you
to give them their food at the proper time.
When you give it to them,
they gather it up;
when you open your hand,
they are satisfied with good things.
When you hide your face,
they are terrified;
when you take away their breath,
they die and return to the dust.
When you send your Spirit,
they are created,
and you renew the face of the ground.

May the glory of the Lord endure forever;
may the Lord rejoice in his works—
he who looks at the earth, and it trembles,
who touches the mountains, and they smoke.

I will sing to the Lord all my life;
I will sing praise to my God as long as I live.
May my meditation be pleasing to him,
as I rejoice in the Lord.
But may sinners vanish from the earth
and the wicked be no more.

Praise the Lord, my soul.
Praise the Lord
Psalm 104:1-35 NIV

Nine-Foot Stake

It was a sunny Saturday afternoon, and we were diving off one of the corners of the Bermuda Triangle. Henson and I were on a self-exploration of a nine-foot stake, and the water a translucent blueish green. We were enthusiastic about having a relaxing, yet exciting day on the reef. We dropped in and off we went into the relatively shallow depths. Immediately we sunk down to about thirty-six feet, where we came across the biggest conch shell I've ever seen, buried between brain coral and the fine sand of the sea bed. We continued around a seven-foot coral wall and there, about fifty yards away, was a nurse shark making his way down the sandy corridor between the reef beds and coming directly towards us! Once he got within fifteen yards of us, he quickly maneuvered over into another coral corridor to stake out whatever food he was lurking for. We continued to swim for the next fifty minutes enjoying the peacefulness of the ocean, the hidden passageways of the reefs, and copious wildlife that occupied our curiosity throughout our dive. Although this sounds amazing, there was a feeling that I couldn't shake while on the dive. I felt honored to be able to be within this environment and have the opportunity to participate in this casual exploration of the reef systems, but there was something quite routine about it. Something more ordinary. Although I enjoyed the idea of it, I was not overly excited to peer over the next corner.

Sully & Henson resting in the sand at Nine-Foot Stake Key West, Florida

Although I appreciated being there, I didn't love being there. And why is that? What caused a shift inside me? Experiencing the overflowing immensity of the open ocean and exploring the grandeur of the Vandenberg radiated so deep within me that going out to the reef was nothing as compared to the gravity of sinking 100 feet deep on a wreck. The reef was wonderful, but it didn't hold a candle to investigating, digging, and trekking into territory unknown that was waiting to reveal itself. Diving the Cayman Salvage was such a rush, and such an amazing experience for a wreck dive. Even though it probably wasn't even half the size of the Vandenberg Wreck dive, the overwhelming feeling of submerging myself around the mysteries and histories of the artifact were potently illuminating.

And this is what God showed me about this experience. It was more than just a "rush." Once we attach ourselves to God, we are opening ourselves to the creator of the universe. That's pretty big! The creator of all things and the source from which all things flow. That said, anyone that fully commits to God has this experience of a purpose bigger than themselves and the sense of meaningful things yet to come for their lives, that God has yet to unveil. Let me put it in other terms. When I go a couple of days without reading the Bible, praying as much as usual, studying the word, or conversing with other Christians, I feel disconnected in my relationship with Christ. The flow, the energy, the spirit of that love is not felt as when I am daily dialed in. I feel sorely disconnected from who God is, and it is an indicator to become dialed back in. Everything can look as though it is beautiful in our lives, and we can still feel the absence of God. We can still have a longing for Him in our heart, one that undoubtedly penetrates the needs of our souls. Just like that reef I was on. It was beautiful and everything around me said this was captivating, but on the inside, my heart was not there. If you have experienced this, I am sure you can relate.

I know I can relate. I've experienced amazing accomplishments around the world, and nothing is as rewarding as when God moves in your life. I've won championships, medals, awards, plaques, and have been popular in some circles. All more emptying than the next. The external looked shiny and abundant, but the internal was severely separated. It is no phenomenon when successful people of all races and social classes experience bouts of depression, suffering, anxiety, suicidal ideation, and bitterness. Because none of these emotions and battles discriminate. They don't care about what is going on in your life or what you are trying to accomplish. Likewise, by attaching our lives to God, we are healed, we grow in spiritual maturity, we live more fulfilling lives, and we evade the subjugation of the emptiness that is in our hearts. We all have busy lives, right? But we prioritize what is important to us.

Saul was thirty when he was appointed King over Israel and reigned for forty-two years. But the Kingdom was torn away from Saul due to his disobedience. Saul was appointed King by the Lord when there was no King in Israel. And because of his disobedience, the Spirit of the Lord departed from Saul.

1 Samuel 15:16-19, 26-29; *"Enough!" Samuel said to Saul. "Let me tell you what the Lord said to me last night." "Tell me," Saul replied.*

17 Samuel said, "Although you were once small in your own eyes, did you not become the head of the tribes of Israel? The Lord anointed you king over Israel. 18 And he sent you on a mission, saying, 'Go and completely destroy those wicked people, the Amalekites; wage war against them until you have wiped them out.' 19 Why did you not obey the Lord? Why did you pounce on the plunder and do evil in the eyes of the Lord?"....26 But Samuel said to him, "I will not go back with you. You have rejected the word of the Lord, and the Lord has rejected you as king over Israel!"

27 As Samuel turned to leave, Saul caught hold of the hem of his robe, and it tore. 28 Samuel said to him, "The Lord has torn the Kingdom of Israel from you today and has given it to one of your neighbors—to one better than you. 29 He who is the Glory of Israel does not lie or change his mind; for he is not a human being, that he should change his mind."

1 Samuel 16:14; *Now the Spirit of the Lord had departed from Saul, and an evil spirit from the Lord tormented him.*

The chasms within our heart will only be filled by the only one who has the providence to fill them; Augustine of Hippo said "Our hearts are restless, until they can find rest in you"

Marker 32

It was the second dive of the day, and we are on Marker 32. The reef system from our drop in point was about sixty yards away in front of the boat, so there was a little swimming to do. We wandered the reef for about forty minutes and decided to head back. We hit all the landmarks, headed back to the boat, and after hitting the last landmark, which was a huge brain coral, we figured we had the sixty yards left to reach the boat. After about fifteen minutes of swimming in the same direction, things were no longer familiar. It was apparent that we were off course, had no idea where we were in our present location, and the water was gradually getting deeper. The beautiful thing about shallow depths is that you can pop up wherever you are and gauge navigation. So that's what we did. We came up from the thirty-five-foot waters and we were directly west of the boat, off about 120 yards.

The current had picked up, pushing us towards the west, and because the current picked up a little bit it also created some fog in the water. Changing the view enough underwater to disorient us. So, why is this a big deal? Why do I tell this mundane story? We knew the current had picked up some on the way back to the boat, but it was light so we didn't think anything of it. And that is exactly how we get side-tracked from Jesus. It is the light currents, the ordinary, the routine things in life that just blur our vision, blur our attention a little bit by little bit at a time until you are yards away from God. We hold conversations, stand in the pulpits, and text back and forth about the huge things that bring us to God and seem to take us away from God. But what about the light currents that slowly take our attention captive until we are no longer fixated in our faith. The slow chipping away of family, friends, kids, video games, television, social media, our own interests, sports, careers, education, religious zeal, and the list goes on. All these things are not necessarily bad, but when God is not the pinnacle focus they distract from relationship and the glory in your life. It is the heart from which our faith is poured. The heart we put into our endeavors. The heart the Lord examines. Let us take look a Solomon.

Crowned to be the wisest man in the Bible, he wrote the books of wisdom and was visited from far and wide by peoples from all over the world. It was wisdom that was granted by God Himself. But Solomon slowly veered away from God.

1 Kings 11:1-4; *King Solomon, however, loved many foreign women besides Pharaoh's daughter—Moabites, Ammonites, Edomites, Sidonians and Hittites. They were from nations about which the Lord had told the Israelites, "You must not intermarry with them, because they will surely turn your hearts after their gods." Nevertheless, Solomon held fast to them in love. He had seven hundred wives of royal birth and three hundred concubines, and his wives led him astray. As Solomon grew old, his wives turned his heart after other gods, and his heart was not fully devoted to the Lord his God, as the heart of David his father had been.*

Today I want to challenge if your heart is fully devoted to God. We get wrapped up in the peripheral elements of life and at times become fully fixated on them instead of our walk with Christ. Another word for fully is completely. Are our hearts and minds completely on Christ? Not partially, not nine tenths of the way there, but fully. Are we busy looking at the elements to the side of us and not keeping God in front of us moving towards Him? We want a full life, but it needs to be full of Christ.

John 14:6; *Jesus answered, "I am the way and the truth and the life."*

John 6:26-27; *Jesus answered, "Very truly I tell you, you are looking for me, not because you saw the signs I performed but because you ate the loaves and had your fill. Do not work for food that spoils, but for food that endures to eternal life, which the Son of Man will give you.*

Conclusion

By Kevin Hill

"Sometimes we have to get wet to understand how dry our lives really are."

I have never been scuba diving. I have never taken a course and been certified to dive into the deep abyss and confront the murky depths and the organisms that call that arena home. I haven't strapped a tank to my back and goggles on my head and traveled to a spot to dive my plan. I have never done it.

So what possible insight could I lend the conclusion of this book? That is precisely the question I asked God. You see, maybe you have gone scuba diving and the words written prior to this closing chapter pulled your interest in close and reminded you of your prior explorations of various bodies of water. Yet many, like me, have not. So, if you have or if you have not, the fact remains GOD has got you covered.

The Tossing Sea

The book of Isaiah gives an amazing illustration of the wicked in contrast to the forgiven.

Isaiah 57:19-20 AMP; *As I create the praise of his lips, Peace, peace, to him who is far away [both Jew and Gentile] and to him who is near!" Says the Lord; "And I will heal him [making his lips blossom anew with thankful praise]." But the wicked are like the tossing sea, for it cannot be quiet, And its waters toss up mire and mud.*

Every day we go out to sea, if you will, into this "tossing sea." The level of wickedness in the world seems to increase every second, with no relenting in sight. How are we to deal with such a reality without faith? The undercurrent of sin is so subtle that the wickedness can make us forget how violent and reckless life really is. It's literally like living on a tossing sea. If we take a moment and look at the nightly news, or to read the latest headlines of your local newspaper, the reality of GOD's words come into focus.

Yet the first portion of this Scripture speaks of peace. That's where faith comes in, and it's what we must dive into. JESUS spoke of keeping us in the world while not taking us out of the world, but keeping us from the evil one (John 17:15). You know, why not just get us out of here when we come to saving faith in JESUS? Why leave us here to deal with such wickedness, mire, and mud? Why do we have to deal with the seasickness of life? With the pain of financial frustrations. Wayward children who test the patience we barely have. Cancer striking family members, disease crippling wonderful people who haven't hurt a soul. These things don't add up, if we are honest with ourselves. Why do such horrific things happen to good people? Why such a tossing sea?

This is where faith ties all things together. Where we believe in God more than we believe the lie. The lie that we are what we are and we can never change. That I control my destiny outside of GOD. That my destiny is determined by me, and me alone. That God doesn't care about me or my situation. These lies sink us deeper in the tossing sea with no gear or oxygen.

All of us were at one point existing this way. Existing in this tossing sea. Some may still be there right now. If you are, please accept Jesus as your Lord and Savior, for HE will save your soul and bring you from existing to living. The oxygen we live by as a disciple of Christ is faith in Him. We will suffocate in this tossing sea if we choose to not have faith. Notice I said "choose." We all have been given a measure of faith, but will we choose to dive in and activate it? It all begins with getting off the boat.

Get off the Boat

Peter is known for many things. I won't assume you know all of them, but I will let you know that he is the only person recorded in the Bible to walk on water besides Jesus. Don't miss that, the ONLY! The tossing sea of a wicked world has been churning up waves for a long time now. So, it is appropriate that Jesus illustrates what He does when it comes to tossing water. He walks on them.

Matthew 14:25-31 NIV; *Shortly before dawn Jesus went out to them, walking on the lake. When the disciples saw HIM walking on the lake, they were terrified. "It's a ghost," they said, and cried out in fear. But Jesus immediately said to them: "Take courage! It is I. Don't be afraid." "Lord, if it's YOU," Peter replied, "Tell me to come to YOU on the water." "Come," HE said. Then Peter got down out of the boat, walked on the water and came toward Jesus. But when he saw the wind, he was afraid and, beginning to sink, cried out, "Lord, save me!" Immediately Jesus reached out HIS hand and caught him. "You of little faith," He said, "Why did you doubt?"*

This account is the challenge that we lay before you. Get off the boat! As I said earlier, I have never taken one dive in my life, but I guarantee you one thing: you can't dive into any body of water unless you get off the boat. We spend a vast amount of time on the boat, with the tossing seas of life making us sick to our stomach. So we see Jesus and make a heartfelt petition to come to Him. He graciously says yes, and we begin to move. As we move towards Him, things began to shift under our feet. The faith to get out the boat has now turned to fear and apprehension as we take our eyes off of Christ outside the boat.

Let me pause for a moment to drop this nugget in your heart. Don't overlook how Jesus was there immediately to catch Peter when he got out of the boat. Sometimes we have to get wet to understand how dry our lives really are. Jesus is calling us, beckoning us to meet our purpose with Him, and we desire the comforts of the boat until those comforts become confinement and they carry us to a place we don't want to be. So, get out of the boat, if the situation gets out of hand, grab His hand, and then commence your faith dive as He guides you.

OK, back to the Scripture. We have to get out the boat. Peter had the faith to get out the boat, but why? So *you* can get out of the boat! We all have our boats. What is your boat? Let me restate it. With all the murk and mire and tossing seas, and you know you need to go to Jesus, what is your boat?

As Peter got back in the boat with Jesus, he was wet. He was the only one who was wet. He was the only one sitting there with an experience that no one could relate to. That's what diving into faith is all about. Taking a dive with the Master Diver and having an experience that is truly a testimony. Faith is an action. It is not faith if it remains a noun. Let me give this a bit of balance. I am not saying for you to dive into any and all things. I am saying that you know the areas in your life that the boat has become your safe haven instead of Jesus. The areas where you desperately need a closer walk with Jesus, but the boat has now become your barrier.

You have to get off the boat. You may be the only one at times, like Peter. Yet getting off the boat allows for **DIVING INTO FAITH!**

References

Jefferis, David. "Christ of the Abyss Statue." Christ of the Abyss Statue | Sea Dwellers Dive Center | Key Largo, FL 33037. Accessed July 2020. https://www.seadwellers.com/christ-of-the-abyss-statue.htm.

Lonne, Torben. "Do Scuba Divers Really Need A Safety Stop?" Last modified January 29, 2020. Accessed May 1, 2020. https://www.divein.com/guide/safety-stop-why-do-i-need-to-do-it/.

Get Involved

Grind Institute

Grind Institute is a pillar within Maximize the Moment dedicated to the furthering of academics, fitness and health motivation. Grind Institute encourages educational progression of all ages to push for individual betterment, self-discipline, knowledge expansion, and healthier living. Grind Institute doesn't seek just students but life learners that are seeking to enhance their daily lives. Partner with Grind Institute today for life-enriching education and opportunities.

GRIND Scholarship Information

Maximize the Moment's Grind Institute Scholarship's purpose and vision is to grant $750 to a couple of hard-working students, an opportunity to further themselves to the next academic level. Through our mission of maximizing what is inside and expounding on all the everyday moments that occur, we hope to fuel the innovation, creativity, excellence, and development of students through this scholarship program. Applicants can email MTM.Inspiration@gmail.com to receive a criteria form or engage with an MTM staff member. Starting in August, forms will be available and application must be received by MTM NLT by 26 April of the current calendar year. The criteria form is a guideline, and students must meet mandatory requirements. Additionally, students may add any prevalent documents that they feel will add strength to the overall package (i.e. reference letters, essays, recognition, etc.)

Missions

Missions are a critical way Maximize the Moment strives to create a difference throughout the world! Through missions we strive to build, catalyze, and ignite change for Christ globally. Missions are a vital way we spread the word and build communities, teams, and individuals, not just within the United States but everywhere and for everyone.

Ambassadors of Christ is a prison ministry that seeks, connects, and ministers to those currently incarcerated. This explosive movement is led by Danny Cox with the help of Kevin Hill, Ricardo Valdez, and Sydney Sullivan. They travel, speak, and testify to bring souls into the Kingdom and spread the love of Christ. If interested, please see the contact page for church, prison, or facility to coordinate a visit!

MISSION

By maximizing every moment in God, we plan on empowering and evolving people around the world through God, community, academics, fitness, and other means of connection.

VISION

Change the world through Jesus, who motivates, Inspires, and empowers this ministry in His name.

Website: MTMinspiration.com

Contact: 305-780-6348

Email: MTM.inspiration@gmail.com

Podcast: MTMinspiration.com/Podcast, Podbean, Apple, iHeart Radio, Amazon Music, Pandora, Tune-In

YouTube: www.MTMYoutube.com

Facebook: https://www.facebook.com/MTMINSPIRATION

Instagram: MTM_Inspiration

Snap Chat: MTM.Inspiration

About the Authors

Motivator, speaker, minister athlete, trainer, and military member, Sully seeks to inspire people from all walks of life around the world to develop, progress, and execute daily. He persists daily to exemplify the highest servitude by giving back to all communities. Examples of programs Sully has engaged in globally are STEM, "Man Up Program," JROTC, "Stay Connected," Ambassadors of Christ Prison Ministry, Red Cross, Big Brother, First Term Airman Center speaker, Military professional development courses, school brown bag programs, family events, AAU development, high school career days, injured veteran programs, and much more.

Sydney Sullivan has spent over a decade in the Armed Forces serving, competing, and speaking. From chef to IT specialist to working in ministry, Sydney Sullivan readily relates to the developmental process and understands what it takes to seize opportunity in the midst of adversity. He currently holds a bachelors in Information Technology Management and is pursuing a Masters in Divinity.

Minister, speaker, and retired veteran Kevin Hill brings a unique global perspective. His travels as a boom operator in the United States Air Force and coast-to-coast ministry (pastoral counseling, teaching, prison ministry, and preaching) all add to his dynamic insight and execution. Kevin lives behind the application and foundational principal of "He must become greater, I must become less" (John 3:30).